UNEMPLOYMENT INSURANCE TRUST FUND ADEQUACY
in the 1990s

Wayne Vroman
The Urban Institute

1990

W. E. UPJOHN INSTITUTE for Employment Research
Kalamazoo, Michigan

Library of Congress Cataloging-in-Publication Data

Vroman, Wayne.
 Unemployment insurance trust fund adequacy in the 1990s / Wayne
Vroman.
    p.   cm.
 Includes bibliographical references and index.
 ISBN 0-88099-101-1 (alk. paper). — ISBN 0-88099-102-X (pbk. :
alk. paper)
   1. Insurance, Unemployment—United States—States—Finance.
I. Title.
HD7096.U5V78   1990
353.0082'56—dc20   90-47790
                                                          CIP

Copyright © 1990
W. E. Upjohn Institute for Employment Research
300 S. Westnedge Avenue
Kalamazoo, Michigan 49007

Cover design by J.R. Underhill
Index prepared by Shirley Kessel
Printed in the United States of America

Acknowledgments

This volume uses a simulation methodology to address questions about the financing of unemployment insurance. It has benefited from the advice, encouragement, and support of several individuals and two organizations. The W. E. Upjohn Institute for Employment Research and The Urban Institute both provided financial support without which the project could not have been undertaken.

Several people familiar with unemployment insurance gave advice, answered technical questions, and made suggestions for improvements in first drafts of chapters. Christopher O'Leary at the Upjohn Institute read all chapters of the report. He also contributed in several ways that improved the quality of the research, as well as the readability of the text. James Manning of the U.S. Labor Department Unemployment Insurance Service and Richard Hobbie of the staff of the U.S. House of Representatives Committee on Ways and Means, both knowledgeable experts on unemployment insurance, also made helpful suggestions on individual chapters. Cindy Ambler and Sheila Woodard of the Unemployment Insurance Service patiently and graciously responded to several questions and requests for data.

Perhaps the largest debt is owed to the professional staff of the unemployment insurance programs in the states. To single out all individuals would be difficult, but key persons in the states deserve explicit recognition. They are: Eugene Innman and John Lundstrom in California, David Bagley and Milton Miley in Florida, Rena Kottcamp in Massachusetts, Jim Kleinschmitt in Michigan, Ann Funeri and Jim Ware in New Jersey, Jim Hemmerly in Ohio, and Bob Gant in Texas. These individuals were helpful in answering questions and providing data that were used in the simulation models.

iii

The Author

Dr. Wayne Vroman is a senior research associate at The Urban Institute. He has directed several research projects and published widely on such topics as money wage inflation, employment discrimination, payroll tax incidence, retirement behavior, and permanent partial disability. In earlier research on unemployment insurance he developed a microsimulation model of benefit payments in the individual state programs. He has also examined a number of other unemployment insurance subjects, such as the program's macroeconomic effects, replacement rates, legislative developments, and program performance in the first half of the 1980s. The present volume builds upon his earlier research on trust fund adequacy that commenced in the mid-1980s. He continues to conduct research on trust fund adequacy and has worked directly with the unemployment insurance agencies in several states.

Policy Summary

This book presents and analyzes the historical background of the unemployment insurance (UI) funding problems of the 1970s and 1980s, followed by a model-based assessment of potential funding problems for future years. Concluding that a serious recession in the near future would cause several states to need UI loans from the U.S. Treasury, the author presents a discussion of a possible new federal role for enhancing UI solvency. "Even if the federal government were not to modify its present *laissez-faire* policy stance," he says, "it might take actions that would affect the risk of insolvency in the states."

In the case of a recession, likely candidates for borrowing would be states whose reserve ratio multiples were less than .5 (Illinois, Louisiana, Michigan, Minnesota, Ohio, Pennsylvania, and Texas, for example). The regional pattern of the recession would also influence which states would become large-scale borrowers.

Under present federal policy regarding UI financing, the states are held responsible for funding their own programs, using any combination of funding strategies (pre-funding, automatic pay-as-you-go financing, or discretionary pay-as-you-go financing). Alternatively, the author suggests, federal policy could encourage the states to (1) achieve a trust fund solvency standard; (2) enact more flexible financing legislation; or (3) participate in a cost sharing/cost reimbursement arrangement whereby reserves from prosperous states are made available to those with funding problems. A cost reinsurance plan would mean the states would pay into a common fund and those with unusually bad experiences would receive payments for part or all of the excess costs due to unforeseeable events. Under a cost equalization plan, states with excessive cost burdens arising from economic factors beyond state control would receive payments from the U.S. Treasury or from a cost equalization fund.

Under cost reinsurance or cost equalization, exclusive state responsibility for UI financing would be ended. Although any such plan would need to address many specific implementation questions and issues, the main principle is that there would be shared responsibility for funding excess costs incurred by the states experiencing the worst economic conditions.

CONTENTS

Tables

1
Background
of the
Financing Problem

State unemployment insurance (UI) pays benefits that provide partial wage loss replacement for the unemployed. It has been an important social insurance program in the U.S. for more than 50 years. Program benefits to unemployed workers provide a degree of income security for many families and enhance the built-in stability of the macroeconomy. Payroll taxes levied on covered employers and paid into trust funds maintained at the U.S. Treasury are the sole source of funding for most state UI programs. In all states the payroll taxes are (partially) experience rated, i.e., benefit claims filed mainly by employees on temporary or permanent layoff influence the tax rates levied on individual employers. The three main objectives of state UI are to provide partial wage loss replacement for individual workers, to enhance the automatic or built-in stability of the economy, and to promote worker attachment with individual employers through experience rating of employer taxes (Haber and Murray 1966, chapter 1).

During the 1980s there were two major developments in state unemployment insurance; an unprecedented reliance on loans from the U.S. Treasury to make benefit payments, and a sizable reduction in the availability of program benefits to the unemployed. Both developments are related to a problem of inadequate benefit financing, which first emerged in the 1970s. Trust fund balances in many states have not been large enough to meet the heavy demand for benefits from eligible unemployed workers. Individual states in this situation have responded in different ways: by borrowing from the U.S. Treasury, raising UI taxes, and/or restricting the availability of UI benefits. Among the states that have incurred UI debts there has been a sharp increase in the pace of debt repayment in the 1980s.

Loans, Debt and Debt Repayment

For more than 30 years following the creation of the state UI programs in the mid-1930s, the system of financing benefit payments with trust fund reserves functioned quite well. Large trust fund accumulations occurred in all states before and during World War II. Following the recessions of 1949, 1954, 1958 and 1960–61, nominal trust fund balances were largely restored to pre-recession levels. In almost all states fund balances proved adequate when benefit payments rose during a later recession.

Prior to the 1970s there were three instances where trust fund balances became sufficiently depleted to necessitate state borrowing. Alaska, Michigan and Pennsylvania secured loans from the U.S. Treasury in the 1950s and early 1960s under loan provisions included in federal UI legislation.[1] In two instances (Michigan and Pennsylvania) the state's trust fund balance never actually was exhausted, so that the loans were not used to make benefit payments. Alaska, which first borrowed in 1955, did use its loans to make benefit payments and had a negative net fund balance from 1957 to 1963. The loans to all three states were eventually repaid after fund balances had been restored to more adequate levels.[2]

Although trust fund balances were generally adequate to pay UI benefits in this period, there was a gradual erosion of fund adequacy caused by increased employment and inflation of the 1950s and 1960s. Between the end of 1948 and the end of 1969, for example, the nominal level of trust fund reserves for all state UI programs increased from $7.6 billion to $12.6 billion. Due to inflation and growth in covered employment, however, total payrolls of taxable covered employers increased from $96.1 billion in 1948 to $365.7 billion in 1969. Thus net reserves as a share of total covered payrolls declined from 7.9 percent in 1948 to 3.4 percent in 1969.[3]

Table 1.1 summarizes information on state trust fund balances, loans, debt and debt repayment over the period from 1969 to 1989. The table shows aggregates of annual data for 53 UI programs; the 50 states plus the District of Columbia, Puerto Rico, and the Virgin Islands. Also included in the table are a business cycle indicator (the unemployment

Table 1.1
Aggregate UI Trust Fund Activities, 1969 to 1989
(in $billions)

	Unemployment rate (percent)	Benefit payments	Tax receipts	Net fund balance Dec. 31	States needing loans	Loans	Loan repayments	State debt Dec. 31	States in debt Dec. 31
1969	3.5	2.1	2.5	12.6	0	0.0	0.0	0.0	0
1970	4.9	3.8	2.5	11.9	0	0.0	0.0	0.0	0
1971	5.9	5.3	2.6	9.7	0	0.0	0.0	0.0	0
1972	5.6	4.7	3.9	9.4	2	0.1	0.0	0.1	2
1973	4.9	4.1	5.0	10.9	2	0.0	0.0	0.1	2
1974	5.6	6.2	5.2	10.5	3	0.0	0.0	0.1	3
1975	8.5	13.0	5.2	3.1	16	1.5	0.0	1.6	16
1976	7.7	10.1	7.5	0.9	23	1.9	0.0	3.4	22
1977	7.1	9.2	9.2	1.0	20	1.3	0.1	4.6	22
1978	6.1	8.1	11.2	4.6	11	0.8	0.3	5.1	18
1979	5.8	9.0	12.1	8.6	3	0.0	1.3	3.8	13
1980	7.1	14.6	11.4	6.6	8	1.5	0.3	5.0	16
1981	7.6	13.9	11.6	5.7	9	1.6	0.3	6.3	17
1982	9.7	21.6	12.1	-2.6	17	5.2	0.8	10.6	23
1983	9.6	18.6	14.5	-5.8	28	6.6	3.9	13.4	23
1984	7.5	12.6	18.8	2.2	19	3.0	6.8	9.5	19
1985	7.2	14.1	19.3	10.1	16	2.6	5.9	5.1	13
1986	7.0	15.5	18.1	15.4	9	2.3	3.6	4.8	8
1987	6.2	13.7	17.8	23.2	8	1.2	4.0	2.1	3
1988	5.5	12.6	17.7	31.9	1	.2	1.5	.8	1
1989	5.3	14.7	17.4	36.9	0	.0	.2	.6	1

SOURCES: Unemployment rates from U.S. Executive Office of the President (1988), table B-32. Data on UI benefits, taxes and net reserves are from U.S. Department of Labor (1983) and Handbook updates. Data on benefits include all regular benefits and half of federal-state Extended Benefits. Data on loans, loan repayments and state debt are based on unpublished summaries from the UI Service of the Employment and Training Administration.

rate) and the annual flows of UI benefit payments and tax receipts. In each of the four recessionary periods covered by table 1.1 (1970-71, 1974-75, 1980 and 1982) total benefit payments responded strongly as unemployment increased. In annual data the peak-to-trough percentage increases in benefit payments for the four recessions were as follows; 1969 to 1971–149 percent, 1973 to 1975–219 percent, 1979 to 1980–63 percent and 1981 to 1982–55 percent.

The experience rating of employer UI taxes operates with a lag. Consequently, when benefit outlays rise in recessions there is little immediate response of tax receipts, and trust fund balances declined during each of the recessionary periods covered by table 1.1. The observed time path of the aggregate trust fund balance reflects the functioning of unemployment insurance as an automatic stabilizer, i.e., benefit payments exceed tax receipts during recessions.

The economic downturn of 1970-71 was rather mild compared to some earlier recessions, and fund balances were generally adequate. Although benefit outflows from state trust funds more than doubled between 1969 and 1971, the two-year decline in aggregate reserves was only $2.9 billion (to $9.7 billion at the end of 1971) and over the next two years $1.2 billion was restored. The aggregate trust fund balances of $10.9 billion at the end of 1973, however, represented only 2.1 percent of covered payrolls, down from 3.4 percent at the end of 1969. Also, to make benefit payments in 1972 and 1973, Connecticut and Washington secured loans from the U.S. Treasury which totaled $94 million. Both states experienced very high unemployment between 1970 and 1973 and their reserves were not adequate to meet the increased demand for benefit payments.[4]

The downturn of 1973–75 was very severe, with the total unemployment rate reaching a peak of 8.5 percent in 1975. This recession also was characterized by a high rate of wage and price inflation. The simultaneous occurrence of high unemployment and high inflation (termed stagflation) caused benefit outlays to increase by more than three times between 1973 and 1975 (from $4.1 billion to $13.0 billion). As benefit payments rose, net reserves fell sharply and reached $3.1 billion by the end of 1975. Borrowing by insolvent UI programs became widespread in 1975 and continued for the succeeding three years.

Table 1.1 shows that 16 different UI programs needed loans in 1975, and over the next three years the numbers that borrowed were 23, 20 and 11, respectively. The volume of loans was actually highest in 1976, the year after the business cycle trough but a year of unusually high long-term unemployment.[5] UI programs with small and negative net reserve balances borrowed $1.9 billion in 1976, as well as $1.5 billion in 1975 and $1.3 billion in 1977. Over the entire six-year period from 1974 through 1979, loans totaling $5.54 billion were disbursed to 25 different UI programs (22 states plus the District of Columbia, Puerto Rico and the Virgin Islands). The loans represented 10.0 percent of total UI benefit payments made during these six years.

During 1978 and 1979, net trust fund reserves increased $7.7 billion. Because reserves had been so severely depleted in the preceding recession, however, net reserves at the end of 1979 totaled only $8.6 billion or .90 percent of total covered payrolls. Thus at the end of 1979 the aggregate net reserve percentage was roughly 43 percent of what it had been at the end of 1973 and only 26 percent of what it had been at the end of the previous decade. Given the widespread incidence of reserve inadequacy manifest during and after the 1973–75 downturn, it is clear that UI programs entered the 1980s in a worse overall financial position than they entered the 1970s. In fact, as shown in table 1.1, 13 programs entered the 1980s with outstanding debts associated with loans they had received in the 1970s.

Back-to-back recessions in 1980 and 1981–82 caused the demand for benefit payments to rise again in the early 1980s. Renewed borrowing commenced in 1980 and peaked in 1982 and 1983, the years of highest unemployment over the entire post World War II period. Loans during 1982 and 1983 totaled $11.8 billion, and the number of programs needing loans peaked at 28 in 1983. Loans also continued after 1983 with $9.1 billion of disbursements from the U.S. Treasury between 1984 and 1987. Only $.2 billion was borrowed after 1987.

Over the eight years from 1980 to 1987, when borrowing was a common occurrence, loans totaling $24.0 billion were made to 32 insolvent UI programs. By year, the number of states needing loans ranged from a low of 8 in 1980 and 1987 to a high of 28 in 1983. The loans represented 19.2 percent of total benefits paid by the states to unemployed workers in these eight years. Loans were roughly twice as important to the states during 1980–87 as they had been during 1974–79 (19.2 percent of benefits versus 10.0 percent respectively in the two periods).

Because so many UI programs entered the 1980s with low net balances, the large benefit outlays of 1982 and 1983 caused aggregate net reserves to turn negative and reach a deficit of $5.8 billion at the end of 1983. The net indebtedness of the 23 debtor programs at the end of 1983 exceeded the positive balances of the other 30 programs by almost $6 billion. This situation had never occurred in the entire previous history of state UI programs in the United States.

Since 1983 the states have made sustained and large-scale additions to net reserves. For the six years 1984 through 1989, net reserves increased by $8.0, $7.9, $5.3, $7.8, $8.7, and $5.0 billion respectively. Tax receipts plus interest income have exceeded benefit outlays by substantial margins in these years. By the end of 1989 the net fund balance across all 53 programs stood at $36.9 billion.

Because the recent build-up of net reserves started from such a low level, however, the total of net fund balances at the end of 1989 was still modest relative to the total scale of the UI programs. The $36.9 billion of net reserves represented just 1.9 percent of total covered payrolls in 1989. This was higher than the reserve percentage at the end of 1979 (.9 percent) but less than the reserve percentage at the end of 1973 (2.1 percent) which proved inadequate to fully cover benefit payments made during the 1973–75 recession. Thus despite the large-scale trust fund accumulations of the 1984–89 period, the level of net trust fund balances at the end of 1989 did not seem to be sufficient to obviate the need for further loans if another serious recession were to follow.

Table 1.1 also shows that debtor programs made large-scale loan repayments in each year from 1983 through 1987. Repayments in these years were so large, ranging from $3.6 billion to $6.8 billion, that state indebtedness was largely eliminated. By the end of 1987, only three states had outstanding debts (Michigan, Pennsylvania and Texas) and the volume of remaining debt, $2.1 billion, was the lowest since the end of 1975. Two years later these numbers had been further reduced to one state and $.6 billion of debt. State UI programs during the mid-to-late 1980s increased their net reserves substantially while at the same time repaying most of their outstanding debt.

The rapid rate of loan repayments observed in the mid-1980s stands in sharp contrast to repayment activities of the 1970s. Of the $5.6 billion in loans received by UI programs between 1972 and 1979, only $1.8 billion was repaid during the 1970s and most of this ($1.3 billion) occurred in 1979. Debt repayment of the 1980s has involved ''old'' debt, i.e., debt incurred prior to 1980, as well as more recent debt.

To summarize: (1) Because of inadequate trust fund reserves, many state UI programs had to borrow to make benefit payments during and after the recessions of 1974–75, 1980 and 1981–82. (2) The volume of borrowing has been higher in the 1980s both in absolute dollar amounts and relative to the volume of benefit payments. Loans equaled 10.0 percent of benefits from 1974 to 1979 but 19.2 percent of benefits from 1980 to 1987. (3) Loan repayments have been much more rapid in the 1980s than they were in the 1970s. (4) Despite large-scale net reserve accumulations that occurred between 1984 and 1989, the net reserve percentage (net reserves as a percent of total covered payrolls) at the end of 1989 was less than it had been at the end of 1973 and many states were faced with the threat of insolvency if there were to be another recession.

Unemployment and Unemployment
Insurance Benefits in the 1980s

Coincident with the serious financing problems experienced by UI programs in the 1980s, there have also been noticeable cutbacks in the availability of program benefits. The cutbacks have affected benefits paid under regular UI programs and benefits for long term unemployment. These cutbacks have occurred despite changes in unemployment which, on balance, would be expected to increase (or, at least, not decrease) the proportion of unemployed workers receiving UI benefits in the 1980s. The changes in unemployment will be briefly reviewed before examining the reductions in benefit availability.

Table 1.2 presents summary information on unemployment for the 40 years—1948 to 1987—with data grouped into four intervals; 1948–59, 1960–69, 1970–79 and 1980–87. Note that average unemployment rates have been higher in the 1970s and 1980s than in earlier years and were especially high in the 1980s. The 7.7 percent average unemployment rate of 1980–87 is the highest rate experienced for an eight year period since World War II. The lowest annual rate for 1980–87 (6.2 percent in 1987) just matches the average unemployment rate for the 1970s.

Labor force growth since World War II has been less rapid for adult men than for other segments of the working population 16 and older. Since adult men experience below average unemployment rates, the growing labor force shares of young workers and adult women have been a factor tending to raise the overall unemployment rate. Note in table 1.2, for example, that while the average unemployment rate for men 25 and older was 3.6 percent in both 1948–59 and 1970–79, the overall rates were 4.6 percent and 6.2 percent respectively for these two periods. From a comparison of the rates for men 25 and older and "all others," it is clear that relative unemployment rates for adult men declined noticeably over the 1948–1979 period.

In the 1980s, however, the relative unemployment rate as well as the absolute rate for adult men increased sharply. In fact, the gains in relative unemployment realized by adult men between 1948 and 1979 have been completely reversed in the 1980s. Between 1980 and 1987, their unemployment rate averaged .616 of the rate for all other demographic groups, the highest relative rate for adult men of all four periods covered by table 1.2. Comparing the 1980s with the 1970s, the average unemployment rate for other labor force groups increased by .8 percentage points (from 8.5 percent to 9.3 percent), while the rate increased by 2.2 percentage points (from 3.6 percent to 5.8 percent) for adult men.

The 1980s have also had a very high incidence of long term unemployment. Table 1.2 shows that the proportion of workers unemployed 27 weeks or longer averaged .160 in the 1980s, whereas in the previous decades the proportion averaged .110 or less. The proportion unemployed 27 weeks or longer has been nearly twice as high in the 1980s as it was in the period from 1948 to 1959.

Table 1.2
Measures of Average Unemployment, 1948 to 1987

	Unemployment rate (percent)		Relative unemployment for men 25+	Proportion unemployed 27 weeks or longer	Ratio of insured to total unemployment
	All persons	Men 25+	All others			
1948–59	4.6	3.6	6.1	.578	.088	.492
1960–69	4.8	3.1	6.7	.457	.105	.417
1970–79	6.2	3.6	8.5	.419	.110	.402
1980–87	7.7	5.8	9.3	.616	.160	.337

SOURCE: All data from the U.S. Department of Labor.

The three unusual aspects of unemployment in the 1980s (very high overall unemployment, high relative unemployment among adult men and the high incidence of long term unemployment) are closely inter-related. Economic developments such as plant closings, industrial restructuring, increased import competition and rapidly declining unionization appear to be more prevalent in the 1980s than in earlier decades and causing large numbers of workers to experience serious problems of adjustment in the labor market. Adult men with extensive employment histories and long tenure at high-paying jobs appear to be particularly susceptible to job displacement and then to experience prob-lems in securing reemployment.

To illustrate the interrelatedness of the three unemployment phenomena, a time series regression analysis was conducted to explain the proportion of workers unemployed 27 weeks or longer (PU27). The primary explanatory variable was the overall unemployment rate (TUR). When unemployment rises, the amount of long-term unemployment also rises. The prevalence of long-term unemployment tends to lag behind overall unemployment so that the regression specification used the lagged unemployment rate (TURL) as well as the current rate. Because adult men are often subject to long spells of unemployment and have experienc-ed variation in their relative unemployment rates, the specification also incorporated an unemployment mix variable, unemployment of men 25 and older as a proportion of total unemployment (UM25TU). Finally, the regression included a correction for first order serial correlation (RHO).

For the period 1949 to 1979, the fitted equation based on annual data was as follows (with t ratios appearing beneath the coefficients):

$$(1) \quad PU27 = -.135 + 1.74TUR + 1.67TURL + .169UM25TV + .766RHO$$
$$\quad\quad\quad (4.6) \quad (7.8) \quad\quad (8.7) \quad\quad (2.0) \quad\quad\quad (5.5)$$
$$R^2 = .914$$
$$\text{Std. Error} = .0115$$
$$1949-1979$$

Equation (1) explained over 90 percent of the variance in the long-term unemployment proportion. When the unemployment rate rises, long-term unemployment responds strongly with large effects attributable to both the current and the lagged unemployment rate. Unemployment mix, the proportion accounted for by men 25 and older, also enters equation (1) significantly, but its effect is quantitatively much smaller than the effects of the overall unemployment rate.

Equation (1) made accurate projections of the long-term unemployment proportion for the 1980s. Over the eight-year interval from 1980 to 1987 the average projection from the equation was .175, which was only .015 higher than the actual average of .160.[6] The standard deviation of the eight projection errors was .0184 compared to the equation's standard error of .0115 for the 1949–1979 estimation period. Most of the explanation for the high long-term unemployment proportion of the 1980s came from the effects of the current and lagged unemployment rate. If the adult male unemployment rate had retained its previous relative relationship *vis a vis* other unemployment rates into the 1980s, equation (1) then predicted the average long-term unemployment proportion for the 1980s to be .168 rather than .175. About 88 percent of the increase in long-term unemployment of the 1980s was attributable to the current and lagged effects of higher overall unemployment rates.[7]

On balance, the combined effects of the three unusual aspects of 1980s unemployment (high overall unemployment, high relative unemployment among adult men, and the high proportion of long-term unemployment) should probably have caused the proportion of the unemployed claiming UI benefits to rise. In fact, the standard indicator of claims activity for the regular UI programs, the ratio of insured unemployment (IU) to total unemployment (TU), declined noticeably in the 1980s.[8] Table 1.2 shows that the IU/TU ratio decreased from .402 in the 1970s to .337 in the 1980s. Thus in the recent period of very high average unemployment the fraction of workers claiming regular state UI benefits declined to its lowest level since World War II.

The decline in the IU/TU ratio of the 1980s has been widely noted. To document the unexpected component of the decline, a multiple regression analysis was conducted. For the period from 1948 to 1979, the IU/TU ratio was explained with three arguments: the total unemployment rate (TUR), the total unemployment rate lagged one year (TURL), and the demographic mix of unemployment (the proportion of total unemployment accounted for by men 25 and older (UM25TU)). When unemployment rises, the proportion who are job losers increases and this raises the IU/TU ratio. The lagged unemployment rate proxies for the effect of exhaustions, and TURL is expected to have a negative effect on the IU/TU ratio. Adult men are the demographic group most likely to collect benefit,[9] so that UM25TU is expected to have a positive effect.

The regression result for the 1949-1979 period (with a correction for first order serial correlation (RHO) and t ratios beneath the coefficients) is shown as equation (2):

$$(2) \quad \text{IU/TU} = .307 + 1.53\text{TUR} - 2.44\text{TURL} + .498\text{UM25TU} + .440\text{RHO}$$
$$(6.9) \quad (3.5) \qquad (5.8) \qquad\quad (5.9) \qquad\qquad (2.4)$$
$$R^2 = .842$$
$$\text{Std. Error} = .0241$$
$$1949\text{--}1979$$

All coefficients have expected signs and all are statistically significant. Over 80 percent of the variation in the IU/TU ratio is explained by the regression.

In equation (2), the net effect of sustained high unemployment is to lower the IU/TU ratio, i.e., the negative coefficient on TURL is larger than the positive coefficient of TUR. Since long-term unemployment and benefit exhaustions have been high in the 1980s, they have tended to reduce the IU/TU ratio in this decade. However, the increase in the adult male share of total unemployment has tended to raise the ratio.

When equation (2) was used to project the IU/TU ratio for the 1980-1987 period, the average projected value was .417 or .079 higher than the actual average of .337. Between the ten years of the 1970s and the eight years of the 1980s, the regression projected the average IU/TU ratio to increase by .025 (from .392 to .417), whereas the actual ratio decreased by .065 (from .402 to .337). There clearly has been a major cutback in the availability of regular UI benefits in the 1980s. Equation (2) suggests that the actual availability of regular benefits (as proxied by the IU/TU ratio) has been about 81 percent of what would have been expected based on program performance over the 1949-1979 period, i.e., the actual IU/TU ratio of .337 is 80.9 percent of the projected ratio of .417.

As of mid-1990, a consensus has not been reached as to the cause (or, more likely, the causes) for the recent decline in the IU/TU ratio. Besides the three factors explicitly included as arguments in equation (2)—the level of overall unemployment, the lagged level of unemployment (a proxy for the effects of exhaustions), and the demographic mix of unemployment—several other factors have also been suggested. Four suggested factors are: (1) changes in the industrial distribution of unemployment; (2) change in the regional distribution of unemployment; (3) taxation of UI benefits; and (4) financing problems experienced by several large UI program in the 1980s, e.g., Illinois, Michigan, Ohio, and Pennsylvania.

There have been long-term trends in the shares of employment and unemployment by industry since World War II, towards trade, finance and services and away from mining, manufacturing and transportation. Because fewer unemployed workers claim benefits in the growing industries relative to the declining industries, the trends can cause the IU/TU ratio to decline, and perhaps at an accelerated rate in the 1980s.[10] A similar argument applies with respect to the geographic distribution of unemployment. Generally, IU/TU ratios are lower in southern and western states, which are growing more rapidly than northeastern and midwestern states.[11] Program benefits have been taxable under federal and state personal income taxes since 1979, and this may have reduced the financial incentives for some workers to apply, particularly second earners in high-income households. The timing of the changes in the tax treatment of UI benefits (partially taxable from 1979 through 1986 and fully taxable since 1987) roughly matches the period of decline in the IU/TU ratio.

Particularly relevant for the concerns of the present investigation is the possible contribution of UI financing problems to the decline in benefit availability. It is clear in state data that IU/TU ratios have declined sharply in several large industrial states that have experienced financing problems in the 1980s. To the extent that financing problems cause individual states to restrict benefit availability (through both formal legislation and changes in administrative procedures) avoiding future financing problems could contribute positively to UI benefit availability in future periods.

The decline in the IU/TU ratio has been a concern of UI administrators, policymakers and worker representatives. To help provide a systematic explanation for this phenomenon, the UI Service of the U.S. Department of Labor has sponsored two research projects, the larger and more recent of which was completed in mid-1988 (Burtless and Saks 1984; Corson and Nicholson 1988). Of the research completed to date, including these two studies, three findings are noteworthy. (1) All agree there has been a major decline in the IU/TU ratio in the 1980s. The behavior of the ratio in the 1980s represents a sharp break from its behavior in earlier decades. (2) A long list of potential contributing factors has been identified. Besides factors discussed earlier (benefit exhaustions, demographic mix, industrial mix, regional mix, taxation of benefits, UI financing problems), changes in the EB program, changed treatment of the pension benefit offset and changes in the measurement of total unemployment in the CPS have also been suggested. (3) No consensus has emerged as to the weighting to place on different factors in contributing to the decline in the IU/TU ratio. This third point is amply illustrated by the cautionary tone of the conclusions offered in the report by Corson and Nicholson (1988, p.117.)

Indicative of current understanding of the causes for the decline is the summary provided by Corson and Nicholson (1988, pp. 117–138). The following list of causal factors is taken from table VI.1 of their report. For each factor they supplied a high estimate and a low estimate of its percentage contribution to the reduction in the IU/TU ratio between 1971–79 and 1980–86. In their high estimates, whose sum fully accounted for the decline, eight different factors accounted for at least 10 percent of the total: (1) industry mix of unemployment; (2) geographic mix of unemployment; (3) taxation of benefits; (4) changes in the CPS measures of total unemployment; and four state-level policy actions which restricted eligibility: (5) monetary qualifying requirements; (6) voluntary separation denials; (7) misconduct denials; and (8) disqualifying income denials. Although Corson and Nicholson did not try to determine how many state policy actions of the 1980s were motivated by UI financing problems, the types of changes which they identified as important are all discussed in chapter 2 of my earlier analysis of debtor state policy actions in the 1980-1984 period (Vroman 1986).

Regardless of the full explanation for the lower IU/TU ratio and the contribution attributable to funding problems in the states, the decline signals a reduction in UI benefit availability in the 1980s. The decline means that state UI is functioning less adequately both in maintaining the income of individual unemployed workers and as an automatic stabilizer of aggregate economic activity.

Besides the reductions in IU/TU ratios which relate to benefits from regular state UI programs, the 1980s have also witnessed reductions in benefits targeted on the long-term unemployed. Benefits from the federal-state Extended Benefits (EB) program were restricted following federal legislation of 1981 which changed the way that EB programs in the states could be activated. [12] Furthermore, the temporary emergency program of Federal Supplemental Compensation (FSC) was smaller and was enacted later in the cyclical downturn of the 1980s than the corresponding program of Federal Supplemental Benefits (FSB) that existed during 1975–1977. Due to differences in the availability of both EB and emergency benefits, annualized real per capita benefits for the long-term unemployed averaged $5545 in 1975–77, but only $2014 in 1982–84. Benefits for long-term unemployment declined much more in the 1980s than benefits from the regular state UI programs. [13]

Indicative of a probable link between UI financing problems and benefit availability are state data on changes in IU/TU ratios in the 1980s. Between 1980 and 1987 the UI programs in the four large industrial states of Illinois, Michigan, Ohio and Pennsylvania were continuously in debt to the U.S. Treasury. In contrast, four other large states, California, Florida, Massachusetts and New York, have been debt-free in the 1980s (except for Massachusetts which completed its debt repayments in 1980). Table 1.3 focuses on unemployment and insured unemployment in the two groups of states during the late 1970s and the 1980s. For comparative purposes, national data are also included in the table.

Unemployment rates in the four large debtor states have been high in the 1980s and substantially higher than they were in the late 1970s. The simple average of the TURs for the four during 1980–87 was 9.7 percent, 3.3 percentage points higher than in 1978–79. In contrast, the four debt-free states with large UI fund balances experienced little increase in average unemployment rates in the 1980s; an average increase

Table 1.3
Unemployment Rates and IU/TU Ratios in the 1980s

	Total unemployment rate (percent)			Ratio of insured unemployment to total unemployment		
	1978–79	1980–87	Change	1978–79	1986–87	Change
Four states with continuous and large UI debts						
Illinois	5.8	9.1	3.3	0.464	0.299	-0.165
Michigan	7.4	11.6	4.2	0.464	0.308	-0.156
Ohio	5.6	9.5	3.9	0.358	0.280	-0.078
Pennsylvania	6.9	8.6	1.7	0.501	0.420	-0.081
Simple average	6.4	9.7	3.3	0.447	0.327	-0.120
Four states with large UI trust fund balances						
California	6.6	7.7	1.1	0.408	0.434	0.026
Florida	6.3	6.6	0.3	0.226	0.175	-0.051
Massachusetts	5.8	5.3	-0.5	0.462	0.540	0.078
New York	7.4	7.2	-0.2	0.436	0.388	-0.048
Simple average	6.5	6.7	0.2	0.383	0.384	0.001
U.S. total	6.0	7.7	1.7	0.379	0.313	-0.066

SOURCE: All data from the U.S. Department of Labor.

of .2 percentage points compared to the national average increase of 1.7 percentage points.

Table 1.3 also shows that IU/TU ratios declined sharply in the four debtor states. The simple average of the declines between 1978–79 and 1986–87 was .120, or nearly double the national decline of .066. In contrast, the IU/TU ratios were not much different in 1986–87 compared to 1978–79 in the four other states, increasing in California and Massachusetts but declining in Florida and New York.

It should not be surprising that IU/TU ratios declined substantially in the four debtor states. Each of the four enacted major UI solvency legislation in 1982 or 1983 to gain financial advantages in debt repayments under terms of the 1983 Social Security Amendments.[14] Benefit reductions were an important part of the 1982–83 solvency legislation in each of the four states. Additionally, three of the four (all but Ohio) had previously enacted legislation to reduce benefits in either 1980 or 1981. These statutory changes undoubtedly contribute to the reductions in the IU/TU ratios observed in table 1.3. To date, no one has conducted research to precisely estimate how much state legislation has contributed to the reduced IU/TU ratios in these states. Corson and Nicholson's (1988) conclusion is that state legislation may account for about one-third of the general decline in the 1980–86 period but their estimates may well have underestimated the size of the effect in debtor states like the four included in table 1.3. Further, they do not draw attention to the federal financial incentives that prompted the state legislation following the 1983 Social Security Amendments.

Changing Patterns of Debt Repayment

After a state UI program borrows from the U.S. Treasury, it will pay off the debt by making voluntary repayments or through credit reductions mandated under statutory provisions of the Federal Unemployment Tax Act (FUTA). States that make voluntary payments control the size and the timing of their payments. In contrast, credit reductions under FUTA take place according to a fixed schedule which commences after a loan has been outstanding on January 1 of two consecutive years, with an initial credit reduction rate (penalty tax rate) of .3 percent of taxable payroll.[15] The penalty tax rate rises as unpaid loans have been outstanding for longer periods of time. The year-to-year increments in penalty tax rates have varied in different past periods and have depended upon the financial circumstances of individual states.

The penalty taxes that ensure the eventual repayment by debtor states are technically tax credit reductions applied against the Federal Unemployment Tax (FUT), whose statutory tax rate was 6.2 percent in 1990. State UI programs must conform to certain federal standards, e.g., in 1990 the tax base must be at least $7,000 per worker, the maximum statutory employer tax rate must be at least 5.4 percent of covered payroll and the state must have an approved method for experience rating individual employers,[16] to receive a FUT tax credit of 5.4 percent which reduces the federal tax rate from 6.2 percent to .8 percent. A debtor state subject to mandatory loan repayment provisions receives smaller FUT tax credits, i.e., 5.1 percent rather than 5.4 percent in the first year of mandatory debt repayment. The credit reductions that ensure debt repayment are applied at a single flat rate to all employers in the debtor state.

The distinction between voluntary and mandatory debt repayment is somewhat artificial since a state can avoid mandatory repayments in a given year if the size of its voluntary repayment equals or exceeds the mandatory repayment required for that year, while at the same time satisfying other statutory financial requirements. In the 1980s there were four financial requirements: (1) repay all current year loans by November 1st; (2) repay any FUT penalty tax (credit reduction) that was due for the current year; (3) not borrow from the U.S. Treasury during the next 12 months; and, (4) have a trust fund balance sufficient to pay at least three months of benefits (for the November–January period). If a state satisfied these requirements and wanted to make the current year's repayment with experience-rated taxes, it could use the proceeds from a proportional supplemental tax surcharge rather than do nothing and be subject to a FUT penalty tax (credit reduction).

The mandatory debt repayment provisions under FUTA were not consistently applied to debtor states in the 1970s. Federal legislation enacted in 1976 and in 1978 deferred the full implementation of the repayment provisions until 1980. In 1980, when the provisions did become fully operative, nine states were subject to penalty taxes. Penalty tax receipts are payable in the year following the year when they accrue.

Loans to insolvent UI programs were interest free in all periods through March 31, 1982. Under provisions of the Omnibus Budget Reconciliation Act of 1981, however, loans made after March 1982 have been interest bearing. Interest is charged on loans that are not fully repaid in the same fiscal year they are received. The rate of interest charged for these advances is the same as the interest rate earned by states with positive trust fund balances, but subject to a maximum of 10 percent per year. The imposition of interest charges began just as the economy was experiencing a major recession. Consequently, most loans made in the 1980s have been interest bearing loans.

Because of the large volume of loans required by the states in the early 1980s it became clear that debt repayment would place serious financial burdens on many states with large UI debts. To ease some of these financial burdens federal UI legislation enacted in 1981, 1982 and 1983 included provisions which lessened FUT penalty taxes (credit reduction rates), and modified the terms of repayment and the interest charges on loans.[17]

It is now clear that charging interest on loans has prompted important changes in loan repayment behavior. Since 1983, debtor states have been very prompt in repaying debt, particularly interest-bearing debt.

Table 1.4 summarizes annual data on loans, debt, and debt repayment in the 1970s and 1980s, with interest-free advances distinguished from interest-bearing advances. Of the $29.84 billion in loans secured in these years, $10.47 billion was interest-free and $19.36 billion was interest-bearing. The outstanding debt remaining at the end of 1989 totaled only $.60 billion, and none of it was interest-bearing debt. Thus, by the end of the period covered by table 1.4, all the interest-bearing loans had been repaid compared to 94.3 percent of the interest-free loans. Despite the fact that all interest-free advances were made prior to April 1982 and all interest-bearing advances were made after April 1982, the latter were fully repaid at the end of 1989.

Table 1.4 also reveals significant contrasts in the methods used to repay the two types of loans. Statutory debt repayment requirements

Table 1.4
Summary of State UI Debt and Debt Repayment Activities, 1969–1989
(in $ billions)

	State debt, December 31			Loans to states		
	Total	Interest free	Interest bearing	Total	Interest free	Interest bearing
1969	0.00	0.00	NA	0.00	0.00	NA
1970	0.00	0.00	NA	0.00	0.00	NA
1971	0.00	0.00	NA	0.00	0.00	NA
1972	0.07	0.07	NA	0.07	0.07	NA
1973	0.09	0.09	NA	0.03	0.03	NA
1974	0.11	0.11	NA	0.02	0.02	NA
1975	1.59	1.59	NA	1.49	1.49	NA
1976	3.40	3.40	NA	1.85	1.85	NA
1977	4.58	4.58	NA	1.29	1.29	NA
1978	5.09	5.09	NA	0.84	0.84	NA
1979	3.83	3.83	NA	0.05	0.05	NA
1980	4.99	4.99	NA	1.47	1.47	NA
1981	6.27	6.27	NA	1.61	1.61	NA
1982	10.63	7.57	3.07	5.18	1.76	3.42
1983	13.37	6.93	6.40	6.63	NA	6.63
1984	9.49	5.74	3.75	3.01	NA	3.01
1985	6.11	4.54	1.58	2.55	NA	2.55
1986	4.81	3.40	1.41	2.29	NA	2.29
1987	2.05	1.54	0.51	1.23	NA	1.23
1988	0.78	0.78	0.00	0.23	NA	0.23
1989	0.60	0.60	0.00	0.00	NA	0.00
All years 1969–89				29.84	10.47	19.36

Table 1.4 (continued)

| | Loan repayments | | | | | Loan repayment rate | | |
| | Interest free | | | Interest bearing | | | | |
	Total	Credit reductions	Voluntary repayments	Credit reductions	Voluntary repayments	Total	Interest free	Interest bearing
1969	0.00	0.00	0.00	NA	NA	NA	NA	NA
1970	0.00	0.00	0.00	NA	NA	NA	NA	NA
1971	0.00	0.00	0.00	NA	NA	NA	NA	NA
1972	0.00	0.00	0.00	NA	NA	0.000	0.000	NA
1973	0.00	0.00	0.00	NA	NA	0.000	0.000	NA
1974	0.00	0.00	0.00	NA	NA	0.000	0.000	NA
1975	0.01	0.01	0.00	NA	NA	0.008	0.008	NA
1976	0.04	0.00	0.04	NA	NA	0.013	0.013	NA
1977	0.11	0.01	0.10	NA	NA	0.023	0.023	NA
1978	0.33	0.00	0.33	NA	NA	0.061	0.061	NA
1979	1.31	0.00	1.30	NA	NA	0.255	0.255	NA
1980	0.31	0.06	0.25	NA	NA	0.058	0.058	NA
1981	0.33	0.32	0.01	NA	NA	0.050	0.050	NA
1982	0.83	0.47	0.00	NA	0.36	0.072	0.058	0.106
1983	3.93	0.63	0.01	NA	3.30	0.228	0.084	0.340
1984	6.84	0.88	0.31	NA	5.65	0.418	0.172	0.601
1985	5.93	0.99	0.21	0.11	4.63	0.493	0.209	0.751
1986	3.59	0.80	0.34	0.11	2.34	0.428	0.251	0.632
1987	3.99	0.93	0.93	0.07	2.06	0.662	0.547	0.810
1988	1.50	0.56	0.20	0.00	0.74	0.658	0.494	1.000
1989	0.18	0.18	0.00	0.00	0.00	0.230	0.230	NA
All years 1969–89	29.25	5.85	4.02	0.29	19.08			

SOURCE: All data from the UI Service of the U.S. Department of Labor.

NA=not applicable. There were no interest bearing loans before 1982, no interest free loans after 1982, and no UI debt during 1969–1971. Repayments rates are measured as the ratio of credit reductions plus voluntary repayments in the current year to the sum of debt outstanding at the start of the year plus loans received during the year.

and financial incentives have combined to produce the repayment patterns observed in the table. Debt repayment provisions require that when a state makes a voluntary repayment, it must be applied to the most recent advance, whereas FUT penalty taxes (credit reductions) are applied to the earliest of any outstanding advances. Thus when states made voluntary repayments in the 1980s, the repayment typically applied to an interest-bearing loan. Financial incentives (avoidance of interest payments) also influenced the states to repay these loans most rapidly.

Note in table 1.4 that the total dollar amount of credit reductions associated with interest-free loans exceeded the dollar amount of voluntary repayments of such loans ($5.85 billion versus $4.02 billion). Credit reductions were the larger of the two means of repayment in all years since 1981, with the exception of 1987 when the two are nearly equal in size at a level of $.93 billion.

In contrast, nearly all repayments of interest-bearing advances were voluntary repayments ($19.08 billion versus only $.29 billion in credit reductions). To minimize interest charges and to avoid such charges altogether, the states paid off these loans very rapidly. In fact, only in 1982 and 1983 did the volume of interest-bearing loans exceed the volume of voluntary repayments of such loans.

The final columns of table 1.4 summarize the pace of loan repayment activities. Annual loan repayment rates are defined as the ratio of repayments (credit reductions plus voluntary repayments) to the sum of debt outstanding at the start of the year plus new loans received during the year. The loan repayment rates were much higher in the mid 1980s than in earlier years. Repayment rates for all loans averaged .045 from 1972 to 1979, .060 from 1980 to 1982, and .445 from 1983 to 1989. The sharp increase in repayment rates coincides with the change in the interest treatment of UI loans. The first year when interest payments were due for unpaid interest bearing loans was 1983.[18]

Table 1.4 also shows the repayment rates for interest-free loans and for interest-bearing loans. For interest-free loans, the simple average repayment rate over the entire 1972–1989 period was .140. The repayment rate for these loans exceeded .50 in one year (1987), and it exceeded .25 in three other years (1979, 1986 and 1988). In contrast, the simple average of the repayment rates for interest-bearing loans was

.606 from 1982 to 1988, and the repayment rate exceeded .60 in the last five years 1984 to 1988.

The lower rate of loan repayments observed for the 1970s was due in part to the fact that loans were interest-free. In an economic environment that had substantial price and wage inflation, each year that repayments were deferred meant that repayment would be less burdensome to the debtor state. Two other factors that reduced loan repayment rates were also operative in the 1970s. First, as noted previously, the full operation of the automatic repayment schedule for FUT penalty taxes (credit reductions) was twice deferred in the 1970s. Second, discussions of cost reinsurance and debt forgiveness gave debtor states perverse incentives to slow their rate of debt repayment. A state would probably need to have outstanding debt to realize any financial advantages from cost reinsurance or outright debt forgiveness.

As noted, during most of the 1980s debtor states faced statutory requirements as well as financial incentives to repay loans quickly. Interest costs would be reduced or completely avoided if interest-bearing debt was repaid rapidly, and FUT penalty taxes were levied consistently on states with debt more than two years old. Table 1.4 shows that even interest-free loans were repaid more rapidly after 1982 than they were in earlier years.

As UI programs developed experience with interest-bearing debt since 1982, a clearcut pattern of debt repayment activities has emerged. States that incur debt repay interest-bearing loans very rapidly. If they also happen to have outstanding interest-free loans from earlier periods, these are repaid slowly. The slowest permissible repayment rate for old debt is to pay mandated FUT penalty taxes. By repaying interest-free debt slowly, a state can accumulate a larger trust fund balance and lower the risk of needing additional interest-bearing loans in the event of a recession. Voluntary repayments of interest-free debt have usually taken place only after all interest-bearing debt was repaid and after the fund balance was restored to a level deemed adequate for most contingencies.

Because table 1.4 combines repayment data from all debtor states the repayment patterns are not as obvious as when data from individual states are examined. Table 1.5 and 1.6 show loans and repayments by state for individual years in the 1980s; table 1.5 covers interest-bearing loans and table 1.6 covers interest-free loans. Considering the carryover of debt from the 1970s as well as loans received in the 1980s, these tables identify 30 UI programs with experience in repaying interest-bearing debt and 21 with experience in repaying interest-free debt in the 1980s.[19]

In table 1.5 there are 100 state-year observations for interest-bearing loans, i.e., times when states received loans. The table shows that for most of these years the states also made loan repayments within the same year. There are only 13 state-year observations where a loan was received but no repayment was made, and six occurred in 1982. Many programs borrowed in these years, but to minimize interest costs they repaid the loans very quickly.

Interest-bearing loans were usually completely repaid within a few years of their initial receipt. Table 1.5 illustrates this with indicators of years when states experienced FUT penalty taxes (credit reductions). To activate a penalty tax assessment, an unpaid interest-bearing loan (like other loans) must have been unpaid in the two consecutive January 1sts following its receipt. The penalty tax is then assessed in the next year. Since the first interest-bearing loans were secured in 1982, the first penalty taxes were collected in 1985. There are only nine state-year observations where penalty taxes are indicated (five in 1985, three in 1986, and one in 1987). As noted previously, all states except Texas had completely repaid their interest-bearing loans by the end of 1987. Texas completed its repayments in 1988.

The usual method for making voluntary repayments is for the program to debit an amount from its trust fund balance maintained at the U.S. Treasury. This reduces the program's gross reserves but leaves its net reserves unchanged. In 1987, however, two states (Louisiana and West Virginia) issued special unemployment insurance bonds and used the proceeds to pay off their interest-bearing debt. These programs made their own loan arrangements rather than relying on the U.S. Treasury to cover their trust fund debt. The states expect to pay off the loans after their trust fund balances have been increased to more adequate levels. This innovative method of bond financing also illustrates the strong aversion felt by debtor UI programs to long-term indebtedness to the U.S. Treasury when the debt is interest bearing.[20]

Table 1.5
Interest-Bearing Loans and Repayments, 1982 to 1988

	1982	1983	1984	1985	1986	1987	1988
Alabama		L,V-F					
Arkansas	L	L,V	V-F				
Colorado	L	L,V	L,V	L,V-F			
Connecticut		L	V	V-F			
District of Columbia	L	L	L,V	C,V-F			
Illinois	L,V	L,V	L,V	L,V	L,V-F		
Indiana		L,V-F					
Iowa	L,V	L,V	L,V	L,C,V-F			
Kentucky	L,V	L,V	L,V	L,V-F			
Louisiana	L	L,V	L,B	L,C,V	L,C,V	L,C,V-F	
Maine		L,V-F					
Michigan	L,V	L,V	L,V	L,V-F			
Minnesota	L,V	L,V	L,V	L,V	L,C,V	L,V-F	
Missouri		L,V-F					
Montana		L	L,V	L,V-F			
New Jersey		L,V-F					
North Dakota		L,V	L,V	L,V	L,V	L,V-F	
Ohio	L,V	L,V	L,V	L,V	L,V	L,V-F	
Pennsylvania	L,V	L,V	L,V	L,V	L,V	L,V-F	
South Carolina		L,V-F					
Tennessee		L,V-F					
Texas	L	L,V	L,V	L,C,V	L,V	L,V	L,V-F
Utah		L,V-F					
Vermont		L,V	L,V-F				
Virginia		L,V-F					
Virgin Islands	L	L	L	L,C,V	C,V-F		
Washington			L,V	L,V-F			
West Virginia	L,V	L	L	L,V	L,V	L,V-F	
Wisconsin	L,V	L,V	L,V	L,V	L,V-F		
Wyoming			L,V-F				

SOURCE: Based on loan and repayment data from the UI Service of the U.S. Department of Labor.
Key: L=Loan, V=Voluntary Loan Repayment, C=FUT Credit Reduction, V-F=Final Loan Repayment

Table 1.6
Interest-Free Loans and Repayments, 1980 to 1989

	In debt in 1979	1980	1981	1982	1983	1984	1985	1986	1987	1988	1989
Arkansas	X	L	L		C	C,V-F					
Connecticut	X	L	L,C	C	C	C	C	C,V-F			
Delaware	X	C	L,C	L,C	C,V	C,V-F					
District of Columbia	X	V	C,V	C	C	C	C-F				
Illinois	X	L	L,C	L,C	C	C	C	C	C,V-F		
Kentucky	X		L	L		C,V-F					
Maine	X		C	C	C,V-F						
Massachusetts	X	V-F									
Michigan		L	L	L	C	C	C	C	C,V	C	
Minnesota		L	L	L	C	C	C	C-F			
Missouri				L		V-F					
Montana	X	V-F									
New Jersey	X						C,V-F				
Ohio		L	C	C	C	C	C	C	C,V-F		
Pennsylvania	X	L,C	L,C	L,C	C	C	C	C			
Puerto Rico	X		C	C	C	C	C	C,V-F	C,V	C,V-F	
Rhode Island	X	L	C	C	C	C,V-F					
Vermont	X			C	C	C	C	C,V-F			
Virgin Islands	X	V	C,V	C	C	C	C-F				
West Virginia	X	L	L	L	C	C	C	C	C,V-F		
Wisconsin				L				V-F			

SOURCE: Based on loan and repayment data from the UI Service of the U.S. Department of Labor.
Key: X=Debtor State at the end of 1979, L=Loan, C=FUT Credit Reduction, C-F=FUT Credit Reduction and Final Payment, V=Voluntary Loan Repayment, V-F=Final Loan Repayment.

Debtor state behavior regarding interest-free debt from the 1970s and early 1980s stands in vivid contrast to the interest-bearing debt. Table 1.6 documents the repayment of interest-free debt through 1989. As noted earlier, just two states (Michigan and Pennsylvania) still had interest-free debt at the end of 1987, while Michigan was the lone remaining debtor state at the end of 1989.

Penalty taxes to repay old unpaid loans are applied to the oldest outstanding loans. Note in table 1.6 that at the end of 1979, 13 states had old debt, incurred mainly between 1975 and 1978. Two completed their debt repayments in 1980 (Massachusetts and Montana), but the other eleven did not and were subject to FUT penalty taxes (levied in 1981). Similarly, four states that were debt free at the end of 1979 but that borrowed in 1980 (Michigan, Minnesota, Ohio, and West Virginia) were subject to penalty taxes in 1983. Altogether there are 85 state-year observations in table 1.6 where penalty taxes were levied. There are just four state-year observations where the only type of repayment was a voluntary payment. For most of the observations involving penalty taxes (68 of 85), the credit reduction represented the minimum that the state could repay while satisfying federal UI conformity requirements. Penalty taxes totaled $5.85 billion between 1980 and 1989.

The number of states that made voluntary repayments of interest-free debt was small in each year covered by table 1.6. There are only 23 state-year observations in the table where voluntary debt repayments occurred. The annual dollar amounts of the voluntary repayments in the 1980s are dominated by one or a few states making final payments to completely repay their interest-free debts. Note in table 1.6 that there were no final repayments in 1981 or 1982. For the other years covered by the table, it is instructive to summarize the dollar volume of final repayments and to compare it to the total dollar volume of voluntary repayments. The states and payments by year were as follows: (1980) Massachusetts and Montana – $239 million out of $247 million; (1983) Maine – $4 million out of $6 million; (1984) Arkansas, Delaware, Kentucky, Missouri and Rhode Island – $310 million out of $310 million, (1985) New Jersey – $209 million out of $209 million; (1986) Connecticut, Puerto Rico, Vermont, and Wisconsin – $174 million out of $340 million; (1987) Illinois, Ohio, and West Virginia – $785 million out of $933 million; and (1988) Pennsylvania – $198 million out of $587 million. For practical purposes, voluntary repayments of interest-free debt in the 1980s have occurred only as the final act in repaying this type of UI debt. Over the eight years from 1980 to 1987, voluntary repayments made in the last year of indebtedness accounted for $1.72 billion or 84 percent of the $2.05 billion of voluntary repayments of interest-free debt.

The preceding discussion of debt repayment patterns in the 1970s and 1980s can be summarized in a few sentences. Debt repayment occurred at a very slow rate in the 1970s but then speeded up dramatically in the 1980s after new loans started to carry interest charges. Even during the 1980s, there continued to be a major contrast in debtor state treatment for interest-free and interest-bearing debt. In most years, in most debtor states, interest-bearing debt was repaid rapidly while interest-free debt was repaid as slowly as possible. Large voluntary repayments of interest-free debt typically occurred only at the end of the debt repayment process.

State UI Funding Strategies

The financing problems encountered by many state UI programs in the 1970s and 1980s can be attributed to a number of factors. Most prominent are (1) the high overall levels of unemployment experienced since 1970; (2) the unusual regional patterns of unemployment in the past two decades; (3) the unexpected costs of federal-state Extended Benefits (EB); (4) asymmetric responses of taxes and benefits to high inflation (taxes are less responsive than benefits in many states); and (5) unfortunate timing of benefit liberalizations in selected states. These causes are discussed in detail in chapters 1 and 2 of Vroman (1986). Although many of the earlier adverse economic developments may be less prevalent in future years, there is no assurance that the future economic environment will be free of recessions and/or inflation.

If states are to avoid a repetition of their recent borrowing and debt experiences, they will need to satisfy one or more of the following three conditions: accumulate a "large" trust fund, have a UI tax system that responds quickly and strongly to reductions in trust fund balances (perhaps supplemented by a response of benefit payments as well), or be willing to enact solvency legislation when trust fund balances decline to what are deemed unacceptably low levels. The three conditions are not mutually exclusive. To the extent that the first two are present—having a large trust fund and a responsive tax (and benefit) system—the third can be avoided—enacting additional tax increases (and/or benefit reductions) in a future recession.

It is now clear that one alternative funding strategy followed by several UI programs in the 1970s and early 1980s (willingness to incur substantial debt for a sustained period) is no longer attractive. The charging of interest on new loans caused debtor states to make prompt repayments of loans secured after March 1982. Since interest-free debt is now largely paid off and future loans will carry interest charges, it is probable that any future loans to states would also be repaid promptly. Thus in a future recession states would be expected to avoid debt and to repay quickly any recently-incurred debt.

In the 1982–1984 period when trust fund balances were generally low and new loans carried interest charges, several states enacted major solvency legislation. Vroman (1986, chapter 2) provides details of this legislation in 10 large debtor states. A question to be addressed in chapter 4 is the extent to which similar state UI legislative activity could be avoided in a future recession if trust fund balances were larger and/or if the UI tax (and benefit) system were more responsive. Before undertaking that analysis, however, chapter 2 reviews the existing literature on trust fund adequacy and chapter 3 introduces the simulation model to be used in the analysis of fund adequacy and tax responsiveness.

NOTES

1. The terms of debt repayment requirements for U.S. Treasury loans are discussed later in this chapter.

2. The periods when the three states had loans outstanding were as follows; Alaska from 1955 to 1967, Michigan from 1958 to 1967 and Pennsylvania from 1959 to 1966.

3. For more discussion of the decline in the relative size of trust fund reserves prior to 1970 see chapter 1 and table 1.1 in Vroman (1986).

4. Estimates of annual total unemployment rates (TURs) based on the Current Population Survey (CPS) are available for 27 states from 1970 to 1975 and for all states starting in 1976. For Washington and Connecticut, the TURs from 1970 to 1973 were as follows: Washington – 9.2 percent, 10.1 percent, 9.5 percent and 7.9 percent; Connecticut 5.7 percent, 8.4 percent, 8.6 percent and 6.3 percent. Washington's TUR was the highest of the 27 state TURs in each of the four years, while Connecticut's TUR ranked sixth, third, second and fifth highest respectively in these years.

5. The number of persons unemployed 27 weeks and longer in 1976 averaged 1.35 million or 1.40 percent of the civilian labor force. The highest previous percentages were 1.20 percent in 1975, 1.14 percent in 1961 and .99 percent in 1958.

6. The projections were made using actual values from the 1980s for the three principal explanatory variables from equation (1) (TUR, TURL and UM25TU) and the error term for 1979 from the fitted equation which was allowed to decay exponentially.

7. A regression of the adult male unemployment rate on the total unemployment rate, the unemployment rate for "all others," a time trend, and a serial correlation correction was fitted from 1949 to 1979 and then used to project the adult male rate from 1980 to 1987. The projected unemployment rate averaged 5.09 percent or .69 percentage points less than the actual average of 5.78 percent. When the counterfactual unemployment mix variable was then used in equation (1) to project the long-term unemployment proportion, the average for the 1980s was .168 compared to .115 for the 1970s.

8. Insured unemployment includes some UI claimants who are not presently receiving benefits—people serving waiting periods and (in some states) disqualification periods. In 1986 the number of beneficiaries represented 88.2 percent of insured unemployment.

9. For example, in the two years 1976 and 1977 the IU/TU ratio averaged .382. Among four major demographic groups, however, the IU/TU ratio for these years was as follows; all persons 16-19—.082, all persons 20-24—.288, women 25 and older—.448, and men 25 and older—.650.

10. For example, among unemployed wage and salary workers in the private sector, the average IU/TU ratio in 1976 and 1977 was .532. The corresponding averages for seven broad industries were as follows: mining—.880, construction—.753, manufacturing—.633, transportation—.638, wholesale and retail trade—.372, finance—.471 and services (except for private household services)—.444.

11. For example, the national average of the IU/TU ratio in 1976 and 1977 was .382. The corresponding averages for the nine Census Divisions were as follows: New England—.433, Mid Atlantic—.441, East North Central—.417, West North Central—.420, Mountain—.319, Pacific—.407, South Atlantic—.297, East South Central—.376 and West South Central—.262.

12. See Vroman (1990) for one discussion of these changes. The national EB insured unemployment rate trigger was eliminated, state threshold triggers were raised, and the computation of the state triggers was modified by removing EB recipients from the calculations. All three changes had the effect of reducing the availability of EB benefits.

13. The calculation summed EB plus emergency benefits in each year of both three-year periods, deflated by the personal consumption deflator from the National Income Accounts and divided by the number unemployed 27 weeks or longer in the same year. Cutbacks in long-term benefits are important to the working poor. Vroman (1990) compares the poverty-reducing effectiveness of UI benefits in 1976 and 1983 and finds that UI benefits caused smaller reductions in poverty among the long-term unemployed in 1983.

14. This 1983 federal legislation is described in chapter 1 of Vroman (1986) and the solvency legislation enacted in the four states is detailed in chapter 2 of the same volume, along with the legislation in six other large debtor states.

15. The basic framework which determines the repayment of UI debt has been present in the Federal Unemployment Tax Act since 1954. Repayment provisions were modified three times by federal legislation enacted between 1981 and 1983. For details of this legislative history see chapter 1 in Vroman (1986).

16. There are 35 conformity requirements that state UI Programs must satisfy, 21 specified by Section 3304 of the Internal Revenue Code of 1954 and 14 specified by Title III of the Social Security Act. A full listing of these requirementsis given in Appendix VIII of U.S. General Accounting Office (1988).

17. The three pieces of federal legislation were the Omnibus Budget Reconciliation Act of 1981, the Tax Equity and Fiscal Responsibility Act of 1982, and the Social Security Amendments of 1983. The provisions in these bills affecting UI loans and debt repayment are described in chapter 1 of Vroman (1986).

18. Technically, the first interest payments were due on October 1, 1982 for 1982 interest-bearing loans not repaid by September 30, 1982. The payment of interest for 1982, however, could be deferred until 1983.

19. There are 15 UI programs with experience in the 1980s in repaying both types of debt: Connecticut, the District of Columbia, Illinois, Maine, Michigan, Minnesota, Missouri, Montana, New Jersey, Ohio, Pennsylvania, Vermont, the Virgin Islands, West Virginia, and Wisconsin.

20. Part of the motivation for issuing state debt was financial, i.e., the interest rates payable on state bonds was expected to be lower than the interest rates charged on U.S. Treasury loans.

2
Financing Issues and Literature

Specifying the level of trust fund reserves appropriate for individual UI programs is not a simple task. This chapter discusses several aspects of the UI financing problem and reviews earlier literature on the topic.[1] The perspective of the chapter is that individual UI programs have the primary responsibility for achieving solvency. As such, there is no discussion of the federal role in ensuring solvency, and consideration of cost sharing and cost reinsurance ideas is reserved for chapter 5. The main areas to be analyzed here are basic funding strategies, the concept of an acceptable risk of insolvency, the 1.5 reserve ratio multiple rule, and a review of earlier literature on trust fund adequacy.

The Financing Problem

The financing problem which state UI programs face is a stock-flow situation where the stock of trust fund reserves acts as a buffer between two flows: an inflow made up of tax receipts and interest income and an outflow of benefit payments. Since the rates of inflow and outflow do not necessarily coincide, especially in the short run, the trust fund reserve is needed to ensure that benefits will continue to be paid in those periods when the benefit outflow exceeds the tax-plus-interest inflow.

The financing problem can be described by analogy with a bathtub where the level of the stock of water in the bathtub at a point in time is like the trust fund balance. It rises or falls whenever the rate of inflow does not equal the rate of outflow. The bathtub analogy, however, is deficient in two important ways. First, the rate of outflow from the UI trust fund is highly variable. Cyclical and seasonal factors cause the rate of outflow to be unstable from one month to the next. The current outflow from the fund may be considerably smaller than the maximum (or capacity) outflow to be experienced in a period of severe recession. Second, there is a strong (but lagged) connection between the rate of outflow from the trust fund and the rate of inflow. Through experience rating there is a feedback effect from increased (reduced) benefit payments to increased (decreased) tax payments. Because of experience rating, an initial change in the fund level caused by a changed flow of benefit payments is followed by an offsetting tax change that (partially or fully) restores the fund balance to its previous level. Under a system of full or perfect experience rating, any change in the outflow will be fully matched by a subsequent change in the inflow.

In the United States, experience rating is practiced in all UI programs except in Puerto Rico. Basically there are two types of experience rating systems. Stock-based systems which are present in 33 programs determine employer tax rates mainly on the basis of individual company account balances and the aggregate state trust fund reserve. In these systems (termed reserve ratio systems), employer account balances and the aggregate trust fund reserve as measured on a set date in the current year (often June 30th) determine next year's employer payroll tax rates. The aggregate fund balance determines which among several tax rate schedules is to be used in the next year and the employer's balance determines which tax rate from that schedule is to be applied. Flow-based systems use actual benefit outflows over a recent time period (or a close proxy such as the base period wages of claimants or, in Alaska, recent declines in covered payrolls) to determine which tax rate from a tax schedule is to be paid by each employer. Typically the benefit outflow (or its proxy) is averaged for three years in determining individual tax rates in these systems. The three flow-based systems are termed the benefit ratio, benefit-wage ratio, and payroll decline systems, and they are found in a total in 19 states.[2]

To help ensure fund solvency, many states also provide for emergency (or solvency) taxes to be levied on employers in addition to the taxes determined through the normal experience rating procedures. Solvency taxes may be assessed as flat rate taxes or as proportional add ons to the experience rated taxes. Typically, the level of the state's trust fund balance as of a certain date determines the size of next year's solvency taxes in both stock-based and flow-based experience rating systems.

Regardless of what system is used to determine employer taxes, all experience rating systems have common objectives: to have the capacity and responsiveness to prevent insolvency during a recession and to replenish the trust fund after the state emerges from a recession.[3] A state can meet these objectives even if there is not a perfect match of benefit payouts and tax obligations for all individual covered employers. The important point is that an increase in the outflow of benefits is eventually matched by an increased inflow of tax receipts.

Funding Strategies

Cyclical fluctuations in the economy ensure that there will continue to be year-to-year variability in unemployment and UI claims. Faced with an uncertain demand for benefit payments, individual states may employ different strategies to cover future obligations. There are no federal conformity requirements regarding necessary levels of state trust fund reserves. A suggested standard for trust fund adequacy, the so called 1.5 reserve ratio multiple rule (to be discussed below), has existed for three decades, but few states have maintained reserves as large as needed to meet that standard. In practice, many states have been able to function with much smaller reserves than implied by the 1.5 reserve ratio multiple rule.

Absent a clearcut actuarial guideline for defining trust fund adequacy, individual states can maintain a trust fund reserve as large or as small as they deem fiscally prudent. States must strike a balance between risks of large-scale borrowing with the associated interest charges if reserves are too small and the opportunity cost (of alternative uses of UI taxes) associated with reserve balances that are too large.

Three distinct UI funding strategies can be identified. Introduced at the end of chapter 1, the strategies will be described here in greater detail. The first strategy can be termed pre-funding. States accumulate a large enough reserve to carry them through a recession without the need for emergency tax increases and/or for benefit reductions. The trust fund balance declines sharply in recessions and then is restored by subsequent experience rated tax increases. The second strategy can be termed automatic pay-as-you-go. Under this strategy, the state builds mechanisms into its tax statutes and benefit provisions that automatically increase tax receipts and reduce benefit outlays as the trust fund balance is drawn down in a recession. The third strategy can be termed discretionary pay-as-you-go. Here the state enacts changes in its UI laws that raise taxes and lower benefits when a recession causes the trust fund balance to decline to an unacceptably low level.

Under all three strategies, there is still a risk of insolvency in the event of an unexpectedly severe and prolonged recession. A large and rapid outflow of benefits can exhaust the trust fund reserve before automatic or discretionary adjustments can restore it. Under a strategy of pre-funding, the insolvency risk is reduced by having a larger fund balance that permits the flow of benefits to exceed the (tax and interest) inflow for a longer period of time. Both pay-as-you-go strategies rely on mechanisms to adjust the rates of inflow and outflow to equalize following an initial increase in the benefit outflow caused by a downturn. Both cause the trust fund reserve to be more stable over the business cycle (and, perhaps, smaller on average) relative to the trust fund reserve under a pre-funding strategy.

Since there is a risk of insolvency under all three strategies, one can ask what is an acceptable risk? A discussion of this question is reserved for the next section of the present chapter. To anticipate one aspect of that discussion, a state may experience some risk of short-term insolvency while following a fiscally prudent funding strategy.

Pre-funding and the two pay-as-you-go strategies are not mutually exclusive. A state may rely on elements of all three in determining its present tax and benefit statutes and its desired trust fund reserve. For example, a state might place primary reliance on a pre-funding strategy but plan to make discretionary statutory adjustments in response to an unprecedented (or catastrophic) level of benefit outlays. Given the inevitable lags in implementing pay-as-you-go strategies, all states experience substantial trust fund fluctuations during short time periods like months, quarters and six-month intervals. For time periods of two years and longer, a pre-funding strategy will allow for a substantial response of tax receipts to a large change in benefit payments. Thus, to some extent the distinction between pre-funding and pay-as-you-go depends on the length of time over which the flows of benefits and taxes are observed. For a long time period such as five years, UI financing could be described as largely pay-as-you-go.

Pre-funding program benefits is the characterization most commonly given to state UI financing and the strategy anticipated by the authors of the Social Security Act of 1935. Originally, most states with experience rating did not permit reductions in employer tax rates until the state trust fund had been built to a level that exceeded the previous years benefit outlays.[4] The key question surrounding the pre-funding strategy is: What constitutes an adequate trust fund reserve? it obviously depends (positively) on the size of the potential benefit outflow and (negatively) on the size and speed of the response of tax receipts to increased benefit payments. Since these factors can vary considerably, two states of the same size could have very different requirements for achieving an adequate trust fund reserve.

One aspect of pre-funding that is useful to emphasize is the potential importance of interest payments in financing UI benefits. During the 1980s Florida, Hawaii, Kansas, and Mississippi have maintained large trust funds relative to the size of their annual benefit outlays. In these states, interest payments credited to the trust funds have constituted a sizable proportion of total trust fund receipts. By state, the share of interest income in total trust fund receipts (interest plus taxes) over the 1980-1986 period were as follows: Florida—.274; Hawaii—.174; Kansas—.144; and Mississippi—.206. The corresponding interest income share across all 53 programs for the same period was only .067.[5]

The automatic pay-as-you-go strategy can involve automatic offsetting responses of both taxes and benefits to an initial change in benefit outlays. The usual trigger for the automatic tax and benefit responses is for the state's trust fund reserve to cross (fall below) one or more thresholds specified in the state's UI statute. Potential tax responses include changes in the taxable wage base per employee as well as proportional or flat rate add-ons to experience rated tax rates. Potential benefit responses include changes in the statutory replacement rate (the percentage that links weekly benefits to previous earnings) and a freeze or a reduction in the weekly benefit maximum.

The most common of the automatic tax and benefit features are solvency tax rate provisions which were present in 28 UI programs in 1988.[6] Three programs had automatic tax base response features in 1988 and eight provided for automatic responses in weekly benefits. Altogether, 34 of 53 UI programs had at least one of the three types of automatic response provisions in 1988.

Illinois amended its UI statute in 1987 and among the changes there were three designed to increase the automatic responsiveness of tax receipts and benefit payments. The law called for a flat rate tax surcharge of .2 percent (of the previous year's taxable wages) to be paid by July 31st of the year whenever the trust fund balance as of May 15th fell below $90 million. It also widened the range of experience rated tax rates. Finally, the law provided for annual increases in the weekly benefit maximum from 1988 through 1992, but also specified recessionary conditions (based on three program indicators) that would freeze or reduce the benefit maximum.[7]

The results of simulations conducted by UI Actuarial Service in Illinois suggest that the new law does not eliminate the risk of insolvency. A simulation of a recession that started in 1989 and subjected the state to a repetition of claims experiences from 1982 and 1983 (a period of severe recession) projected total borrowing of about $1 billion which was then fully repaid within eighteen months. For comparative purposes, it should be noted that Illinois borrowed $3.1 billion between 1980 and 1984. Thus, in the face of a very serious recession the automatic pay-as-you-go features of the 1987 law appear to have greatly reduced the scale of needed borrowing, but they have not completely eliminated the possible need to borrow.[8]

Proponents of automatic pay-as-you-go financing believe it has two advantages as a funding strategy. First, when compared to pre-funding, it avoids the need to build as large a trust fund reserve and probably results in a smaller average fund balance over the business cycle.[9] Second, because the provisions to change taxes and benefits are activated automatically, the problems associated with legislative delays are avoided.

A drawback of automatic pay-as-you-go financing is the risk of using it in good times but not sticking with it in recessions. The experiences of Texas and Louisiana in 1982 and 1983 illustrate this problem. Both states revised their solvency tax statutes in the midst of a recession in order to lessen the tax increases to be incurred by their employers.[10] The actions meant that taxes did not respond as strongly as implied by the previous laws, but it was felt that the 1982-83 actions were necessary to lessen the hardships on employers that the larger tax increases would have caused.

This issue is likely to arise in any recession when business profits are already low and to be a bigger problem the more serious the recession. Of course it is precisely during a major recession that large tax increases (and benefit reductions) are needed under an automatic pay-as-you-go strategy since there are large benefit outflows from a trust fund that has been deliberately kept at a low level prior to the recession.

Discretionary pay-as-you-go financing is a funding strategy that relies on new legislative enactments to avoid or reduce insolvency problems in a recession. States can change many aspects of benefits and taxes in order to restore the trust fund reserve. Besides changes in the tax base, the tax rate and weekly benefits already noted there are several other tax and benefit changes that can be considered. Other tax changes include widening the range of experience rated tax rates, levying special assessments on negative balance employers and restricting "writeoff" provisions for negative balance employers.[11] Other benefit changes include reducing maximum potential benefit duration, increasing the waiting period, increasing monetary qualification requirements and increasing the disqualification penalties for nonmonetary issues such as voluntary quits, discharge for misconduct, disqualifying income and availability for work. States that have enacted important solvency legislation in the 1980s have typically modified several tax and benefit provisions in their UI laws.[12]

As a funding strategy, discretionary pay-as-you-go will be more successful if legislation can be agreed to and enacted quickly. Often the legislative package enacted will contain both benefit reductions and tax increases. When legislation entails long lags and trust fund reserves are low, the risk of insolvency rises. To the extent that the state does not pre-fund or enact strong automatic pay-as-you-go provisions, it will have to place greater reliance on a discretionary pay-as-you-go strategy.

One way to compare the relative merits of the three funding strategies is to evaluate them from the perspective of the overall objectives of unemployment insurance. State UI is often described as having three primary objectives: (1) to provide partial wage loss replacement (or income maintenance) to unemployed workers and their families; (2) to provide automatic or built-in stability to the macro economy; and (3) to encourage employers to stabilize employment through the experience rating of UI taxes.[13] Relative to pre-funding, the pay- as-you-go strategies would seem to be inferior in two ways. First, each provides less counter-cyclical stimulus than pre-funding, regardless of the mix of pay-as-you-go tax increases versus benefit reductions used to restore the trust fund balance. Second, to the extent that pay-as-you-go strategies rely on benefit reductions to restore the trust fund, they are inferior to pre-funding in achieving the income maintenance objective of UI. Pre-funding has advantages in achieving both the income maintenance and automatic stabilization objectives of unemployment insurance.

Acceptable Risk

Because the future liability to pay UI benefits has elements that are difficult to forecast, a state does not know with certainty how large its trust fund reserve should be. The depth and duration of recessions are primary factors that cause variability in the trust fund outflow. Funds must be adequate to cover the outflow until the revenue side responds.

One approach for specifying fund adequacy is to argue that fund balances must be large enough to ensure that no borrowing will occur regardless of the size of any future recession. In effect, the fund balance would be large enough to ensure a zero risk of insolvency, i.e., the fund balance never going to a zero level. Predicting the depth of a future recession and the size of the associated benefit outflow poses serious problems for UI programs. To guard against borrowing under any conceivable future contingency, a state would need to have a very large trust fund reserve, a very responsive tax generation system, and/or an excellent forecasting capability in order to enact tax and benefit changes at the appropriate time.

Under present UI law, the tax revenues deposited in state trust funds can have only one possible use: to pay cash benefits to UI claimants. Monies that potentially could be collected as UI taxes have several alternative (public and private) uses. These alternative uses are foreclosed once UI taxes have been levied and deposited in the trust fund. Since UI programs can borrow from the U.S. Treasury to pay benefits when trust funds are depleted, it would be irrational to build trust funds to levels that completely obviated the need for U.S. Treasury loans.

Most states have, in fact, resorted to U.S. Treasury loans in recent years. Between 1972 and 1987, 37 states plus the District of Columbia, Puerto Rico, and the Virgin Islands obtained loans. If the loans are small and indebtedness lasts for only short periods, the utilization of loans is a rational policy and a preferred alternative to the accumulation of needlessly large UI trust fund reserves.

Much of the borrowing that occurred between 1972 and 1987 was small and short term (as the terms are to be defined below). As noted in chapter 1, borrowing activities in these 16 years fell into two major episodes: the first associated with the recession of the mid-1970s, and the second associated with the back-to-back recessions of 1980 and 1981–82. Twenty-five jurisdictions borrowed in the 1970s and roughly half completed their loan repayments by the end of 1980. In the 1980–87 period, 14 of the 32 jurisdictions that borrowed completed their debt repayments within the following two years. It is also clear that loan repayments have been much more rapid since April 1982 when new loans started to carry interest charges.

Define as "small" an amount of borrowing that is less than 1 percent of covered wages and that encompasses all borrowing that occurs during a recession. Although an arbitrary size designation, this scale of borrowing is usually small enough to permit full loan repayment during a subsequent economic recovery without the need to enact major legislation that raises taxes and/or reduces benefits. Nine of the 25 jurisdictions that borrowed between 1972 and 1979 required "small" loans.[14] During the 1980 to 1987 period, "small" loans were disbursed to 18 of the 32 jurisdictions.[15] Typically, these loans were needed for a short period at the end of the recession, and they were repaid promptly in the ensuing recovery, partly from the effects of modest changes in UI tax and benefit statutes. Utilizing loans of this scale can be justified as a prudent policy.

One can define an acceptable risk of insolvency as having two elements: a measurable probability of insolvency, and small-scale borrowing while insolvent. The risk should be measured over an entire business cycle or even longer if economic downturns are as closely spaced as they were in 1980 and 1981–82. Although it is arbitrary, one specific definition of acceptable risk would be as follows: a UI program has a 25 percent chance of needing a "small" loan where a small loan is less than 1 percent of covered wages. As noted, 9 jurisdictions and 18 jurisdictions, respectively, received loans of this scale during the 1972–79 and 1980–87 periods. When experiences of the two periods are combined, they yield an overall average 25 percent chance of needing loans of this scale per recessionary episode.[16]

Under this specific definition of acceptable risk, one can estimate the volume of U.S. Treasury loans that would be needed over a business cycle. Using the 1972–79 and 1980–87 periods as examples one can select a base year from each period to measure covered wages, e.g., 1975 and 1984. If every UI program had the same 25 percent chance of insolvency and if small loans to such programs averaged .5 percent of current wages (the midpoint between 0 and 1 percent), the total volume of small loans in the two periods would have been $.7 billion and $1.7 billion, respectively.[17] Comparing these amounts to the actual loan totals for the two periods ($5.5 billion and $24.0 billion), it is clear that with this specific definition of acceptable risk many states have been exposed to much larger risks.

While many states have needed only "small" loans to help finance benefit payments in recent recessions, it is obvious that the major share of U.S. Treasury loans has gone to states that have experienced large-scale and long-term indebtedness. This point is vividly illustrated with data covering the entire 1972–1987 period. Over these 16 years there were 12 programs that had had UI debts in 10 or more consecutive years.[18] Their loans totaled $17.4 billion or 59 percent of all loans disbursed between 1972 and 1987. An additional 11 states had had UI debts in five to nine consecutive years.[19] Loans to states with UI debts in five or more consecutive years totaled $27.8 billion or 94 percent of all loans for this period. The bulk of U.S. Treasury loans has gone to programs with chronic problems of UI financing.

Although borrowing was widespread during both 1972–79 and 1980–87, 13 UI programs were able to avoid borrowing over this entire period. One analysis identified three important factors associated with debt avoidance.[20] (1) The states entered recessions with larger than average trust fund balances. (2) When trust funds were drawn down these states enacted legislation promptly to raise taxes and (in some instances) reduce benefit outlays.[21] (3) States avoiding the need to borrow typically experienced favorable economic events such as low unemployment and a high rate of economic growth. In the past, active policies and favorable economic events have both contributed to debt avoidance.

Since new loans from the U.S. Treasury carry interest charges, the states now feel more political and economic pressure to avoid large-scale indebtedness than they did prior to April 1982. On the other hand, the states must incur some risks of borrowing to avoid accumulating needlessly large trust fund balances. Thus, a state's problem can be stated as follows: it cannot completely avoid the risk of borrowing, but it wants to avoid large-scale borrowing. One specific strategy for incurring an acceptable risk of insolvency that was discussed here would be for a UI program to incur a 25 percent probability of needing a small loan, i.e., a loan equaling 1 percent or less of wages. If this situation had prevailed during the 1980–87 period, total loans would have fallen into the $1–3 billion range rather than the $24.0 billion that was required.[22] Achieving this level of acceptable risk would have resulted in a greatly reduced volume of loans to insolvent UI programs.

The 1.5 Reserve Ratio Multiple

As a guideline for assessing the adequacy of trust fund reserves, UI policymakers and practitioners frequently measure their fund balance in terms of a "reserve ratio multiple" or simply a reserve multiple. This measure provides a rule of thumb useful for gauging the size of reserves relative to the potential demand for benefits that could occur in a recession. The reserve ratio multiple was first developed at the U.S. Department of Labor, but it became more widely known after being examined and publicized by a benefit financing committee of ICESA, the Interstate Conference of Employment Security Agencies (1959). The multiple is a quotient that is computed from two ratios. The denominator is UI benefit payments as a percentage of total covered payrolls in the highest cost 12-month period (not necessarily a calendar year), while the numerator is total net reserves at the end of the current year expressed as a percentage of total covered payrolls for the year. The numerator is commonly called the reserve ratio. If, for example, a hypothetical state's highest cost year had benefit outlays equal to 2 percent of total payrolls, and if current payrolls were $30 billion, it could expect to pay out as much as $600 million in benefits should the current year have a recession as serious as that of the high-cost year.

The ICESA committee recommended that a reserve ratio multiple of from 1.5 to 3.0 was needed for trust fund adequacy. Although neither ICESA nor the U.S. Department of Labor has formally adopted a specific numeric standard to be used by UI programs in judging fund adequacy, a 1.5 reserve multiple is often used as a guideline in assessments of minimum reserve adequacy. The state in the previous hypothetical example would need a trust fund reserve of $900 million to meet this actuarial guideline.

In developing the 1.5 reserve multiple guideline, the ICESA committee utilized benefit cost data from the recessions of 1949, 1954, and 1958. There were three important elements in the committee's analysis (ICESA 1959, p. 22). (1) The cost rate measured benefits as a percentage of total payrolls, not as an absolute dollar amount or as a percentage of taxable payrolls. The committee reasoned that measuring benefits relative to total payrolls provides a more reliable cost indicator than the other two because it accounts for cost changes that arise from changing employment levels and changing levels of money wages. (2) In the three recessions studied, the heaviest drains on trust funds occurred over periods of about 12 months (periods that did not always coincide with given calendar or fiscal years), and total recession-related outlays were about one and one-half times the costs incurred in the highest cost, 12-month period. (3) Under this analysis, if a state achieves a 1.5 multiple before the onset of a recession, it would have sufficient reserves to last through the recession without exhausting the trust fund and without needing to increase taxes until the subsequent economic recovery has commenced. This level of reserves would allow the UI program to provide the greatest amount of countercyclical stimulus, i.e., benefits rise in the recession but taxes do not respond until the recovery has set in.

From the perspective of the 1980s, three critical comments about the ICESA committee's reasoning can be offered. (1) The past may not provide useful guidance in planning for future high-cost, 12-month periods. Future high-cost years will deviate from previous high-cost years if the level of state unemployment is different, if UI eligibility and/or potential benefit duration are different, or if the level of weekly benefits (relative to weekly wages) is different. (2) The multiplier of 1.5 that relates total recession-related costs to costs in the high-cost year may be incorrect. In both the mid-1970s and the 1980s, recessions have been longer than they were prior to 1960. (3) The 1.5 multiple ignores the responses of taxes to the decline in the UI trust fund balance. This response varies from state to state, and in all states it is larger in recessions of longer duration. These considerations imply that the 1.5 multiple could give misleading signals when applied to specific circumstances.

Another limitation of the 1.5 reserve ratio multiple guideline is suggested by the following example. Consider the hypothetical state of the earlier discussion with covered payrolls of $30 billion and a high-cost rate equal to 2 percent of payrolls. If the UI fund satisfied the 1.5 multiple the current balance would be $900 million. Further, assume that the tax and benefit flows are initially equal at 1 percent of payrolls (and that interest accruals are small enough to be ignored).

If the state now experiences a serious recession and the benefit outflow from the trust fund increases to 2 percent of payrolls, the annual outflow would increase from $300 million to $600 million. Suppose further that the benefit outflow remains at this high-cost rate for three years and that tax rates do not respond as the fund balance declines. Even though the benefit costs in this recession are three times (not 1.5 times) the single year's high costs, the fund balance does not reach zero until the end of the third year of recession. Any lessening of the benefit payout rate or any response of taxes in the second or third year would cause the fund balance to be positive at the end of year three.

Obviously, many other time paths of taxes and benefits could be hypothesized, and some would cause insolvency to occur before the end of year three. The point of the example is to show the importance of the initial inflow and outflow in determining the risk of insolvency. The fund balance must be large enough to cover the increment in the benefit outflow that occurs in the recession, not the total level of costs. Under the 1.5 multiple guideline, the $900 million initial trust fund balance is large enough to cover three years of incremental costs (at $300 million per year) where each year has the full increment (1 percent of payrolls) over base period costs.

The 1.5 multiple is a conservative fiscal guideline. If a state satisfies the guideline it can experience a prolonged period of high costs and still avoid insolvency even when its tax structure responds only slowly to increased benefit outflows. Many UI practitioners regard the 1.5 reserve multiple as a desirable target to strive for, but feel that insolvency can be avoided with fund balances of much smaller size. Since the mid-1970s, very few states have achieved fund balances that satisfy the 1.5 reserve multiple guideline.

Table 2.1 provides summary data on reserve ratio multiples from 1969 to 1989. Because the UI program in the Virgin Islands started in the mid-1970s, it has been excluded from the table. Trust fund reserves are measured as net reserves (total reserves less outstanding loans) at the end of the indicated years. Three years (1969, 1973, and 1979) are prerecession years. Major decreases in reserve multiples occurred during 1969–73 and again during 1973–79. Over the decade from 1969 to 1979,

Table 2.1
State UI Program Reserve Ratio Multiples, 1969 to 1989

End of year	Number of states – (reserve ratio / 12 month high-cost ratio)							Median reserve ratio multiple	Multiple for U.S.
	Negative	0–.49	.5–.99	1.0–1.49	1.5–1.99	2.0–2.99	3.0+		
1969	0	0	1	16	15	12	8	1.82	1.68
1973	1	4	14	12	12	8	1	1.35	1.04
1979	9	13	16	12	2	0	0	.64	.41
1989	0	10	22	17	3	0	0	.91	.82

SOURCES: U.S. Department of Labor (1983) and the Financial Handbook update for 1989. Computations of reserve ratio multiples for 1969 and 1989 done at the Urban Institute. All data refer to the 50 states plus the District of Columbia and Puerto Rico.

the number of programs (out of 52) with reserve ratio multiples of 1.5 or larger decreased from 35 to just 3. Conversely, the number with multiples less than 1.0 increased from 1 (Michigan) to 38. The summary measures in table 2.1 (the median multiple and the multiple for the U.S.) indicate that trust fund reserves at the end of 1979 were only one-third to one-quarter of what they had been 10 years previously when assessed using this particular actuarial standard.

As noted in chapter 1, substantial trust fund increases were realized by UI programs between 1983 and 1989. As a result, the aggregate fund balance at the end of 1989 was $28.3 billion higher than it had been at the end of 1979 ($36.9 billion versus $8.6 billion). From table 2.1, however, note that the aggregate U.S. reserve ratio multiple only increased from .41 to .82 over the 1980–89 period. Because covered wages increased by 107 percent between 1979 and 1987, net reserves had to increase by 107 percent just to maintain the aggregate reserve multiple at its 1979 level.

Based on experiences from the 1970s and 1980s it is clear that the reserve ratio multiple is a useful construct for identifying UI programs that may experience insolvency. Table 2.2 presents data on the distribution reserve multiples at the end of 1973 and 1979. For both the 1974–79 and the 1980–87 periods, the table also shows the total number of states that borrowed and the number that were "major" borrowers, i.e., needing loans that exceeded 1 percent of covered payrolls (as of 1975 and 1984, respectively). As with table 2.1, this table also summarizes the experiences of 52 programs (but not the Virgin Islands, which borrowed in both periods and was a major borrower during 1974–79).

The probability of insolvency was strongly associated with the level of the reserve ratio multiple in both the 1970s and the 1980s. All five programs with multiples below .5 in 1973 needed loans between 1974 and 1979, and all five were major borrowers. Of the 14 with multiples between .5 and .99, 12 needed loans and 8 were major borrowers. Among those with multiples of 1.5 or larger, only 2 of 21 needed any loans and just 1 (the District of Columbia) was a major borrower.

Table 2.2
Distribution of Reserve Ratio Multiples and UI Program Borrowing in the 1970s and 1980s

Borrowing status 1974–1979	Reserve ratio multiples at end of 1973						
	Negative	0–.49	.5–.99	1.0–1.49	1.5–1.99	2.0+	Total
No. of programs	1	4	14	12	12	9	52
Borrowers	1	4	12	5	2	0	24
Major borrowers	1	4	8	1	1	0	15
Proportion borrowers	1.00	1.00	.86	.42	.08	.00	.46
Proportion major borrowers	1.00	1.00	.57	.08	.08	.00	.29

Borrowing status 1980–1987	Reserve ratio multiples at end of 1979						
	Negative	0–.49	.5–.99	1.0–1.49	1.5–1.99	2.0+	Total
No. of programs	9	13	16	12	2	0	52
Borrowers	8	11	10	2	0	NA	31
Major borrowers	2	6	5	1	0	NA	14
Proportion borrowers	.89	.85	.62	.17	.00	NA	.60
Proportion major borrowers	.22	.46	.31	.08	.00	NA	.27

SOURCE: Data on loans from the UI Service of the U.S. Department of Labor (1988b). Loans in the 1970s and 1980s refer to 1974–1979 and 1980–1987 respectively and are measured as a percent of covered wages in 1975 and 1984 respectively. Large loans are defined as loans exceeding 1 percent of covered wages. All data refer to 50 states plus the District of Columbia and Puerto Rico.

NA=Not applicable as no program had a reserve ratio multiple in this range.

The probability of insolvency and the probability of major borrowing in the 1980–87 period were also closely tied to the reserve ratio multiples at the end of 1979. Both probabilities decline sharply as one moves from left to right in the indicated rows of table 2.2. For example, the probability of borrowing was .89 for states that entered the 1980s with negative net reserves, but it was only .17 for states whose reserve multiples fell into the 1.0–1.49 range.

Three other aspects of table 2.2 should also be noted. First, observe that for a given range of reserve multiples the probability of borrowing was much lower in 1980–87 than in 1974–79. In the 1.0–1.49 range, for example, the probability of insolvency was .42 in 1974–79, but only .17 in 1980–87. For a given reserve multiple, states were much less likely to experience insolvency in the 1980s than in the 1970s. Much of the difference is due to the increased costs of indebtedness in the 1980s and increased certainty of incurring those costs in the 1980s. Because states face the prospect of paying interest on UI loans (unless they make rapid loan repayments), they have been more willing to enact solvency legislation in the 1980s when fund balances have been reduced towards zero.

Second, although the probability of insolvency was lower during 1980–87 than during 1974–79 within each range of reserve multiples in table 2.2, the overall probability was higher (.60 versus .46). This is another indication of the loss of reserve adequacy that occurred between 1973 and 1979. When the 1980–87 borrower proportions were applied to the 1973 distribution of reserve ratio multiples, the constructed borrower proportion was .29. The difference between the constructed proportion of .29 and the actual proportion of .60 helps to illustrate the decline in reserve adequacy in the mid- to late-1970s.

Third, although UI programs entered the 1980s with much lower reserve ratio multiples than at the end of 1973, the proportions that were major borrowers were essentially the same in the two periods (.29 in 1974–79 versus .27 in 1980–87). States were more willing to act to avoid major borrowing, but because 1979 reserves were so low, the dollar amount of large-scale borrowing was much higher in the 1980s.[23]

Overall, the data in table 2.2 show that reserve ratio multiples are useful (but not infallible) for judging the probability of insolvency in individual states. The 1.5 reserve multiple guideline continues to be used at the U.S. Department of Labor in its assessments of reserve adequacy. An illustration of this is provided by an Unemployment Insurance Program Letter on reserve adequacy sent to the states in 1981. After noting there is no single definition of reserve adequacy, this document stresses that the 1.5 multiple provides "an indication of a base minimum of reserve adequacy" (U.S. Department of Labor 1981, p. 2). It is interesting to note in table 2.2 that 19 of 50 UI programs that fell below this "base minimum" in 1979 did not experience insolvency in the subsequent recessions of 1980 and 1981–82. Of the 19 that did not borrow between 1980 and 1987, however, 10 entered the 1980s with reserve multiples of at least 1.0.

Two final points about UI program reserves at the end of the 1980s should be offered. First, total net reserves at the end of 1989 fell far short of the level suggested by the 1.5 reserve ratio multiple rule. To bring total net reserves up to the level that would yield a reserve multiple of 1.0 in each state would have required an increase of $6.7 billion above the actual 1989 level of $36.9 billion (to $43.6 billion). Achievement of a 1.5 reserve ratio multiple in all 53 programs would have required net reserves to increase by $28.5 billion (to $65.4 billion). Since only 2 of 14 programs with 1979 reserve multiples of 1.0 or larger received U.S. Treasury loans between 1980 and 1987, it seems clear that achievement of the 1.0 reserve multiple threshold is a much higher priority (as well as being more feasible) than achievement of the 1.5 multiple for programs with lower levels of net reserves.

Second, several UI programs faced the risk of insolvency at the end of 1989. To give a rough idea of the magnitude of the risks, two hypothetical borrowing probabilities have been calculated. Suppose a recession had started in 1988 and it had the same time profile as the downturn and subsequent economic recovery of the 1980–87 period. Then one could use the 1989 distribution of reserve ratio multiples along with the 1980-87 borrowing proportions (in table 2.2) to calculate aggregate borrowing proportions across the 52 UI programs. The calculated proportions, .46 for the proportion needing to borrow and .23 for the proportion needing major loans, suggested that 24 states would need loans and 12 would need major loans. Although this calculation ignores many specific details for individual UI programs, it strongly suggests that additional trust fund building above the levels that existed at the end of 1989 is needed if the programs are to achieve the level of acceptable risk discussed earlier in this chapter, i.e., a .25 chance of needing a loan smaller than 1 percent of covered wages.

Earlier Literature on Fund Adequacy

Although it has been obvious since the mid-1970s that UI programs are having funding problems, this has not stimulated a substantial literature on trust fund adequacy. From earlier research, mainly supported by the UI Service of the U.S. Department of Labor and by the National Commission on Unemployment Compensation, four analyses of fund adequacy have been selected for review. Because they followed contrasting methodologies, however, the four cannot easily be compared. The approach taken here is to summarize each study and then to offer some concluding comments.

An analysis of UI trust funds was conducted by Bowes, Brechling, and Utgoff (1980). They recognized three important components in a state's utility function for determining the optimal level of the trust fund reserve. (1) Because of the opportunity cost of monies held as trust fund reserves, utility falls as the average fund balance increases. (2) An increase in the probability of insolvency lowers utility. This probability falls as the average fund balance is higher and as the variance in the fund balance is lower. (3) States, even those that rely most heavily on experience rating, can choose to exercise a high degree of tax smoothing, i.e., maintaining year-to-year stability in their tax rates. As the degree of tax smoothing increases, the UI program exerts a greater countercyclical impact and utility is increased.

Key elements in this analysis are the parameters of the state's UI tax schedule (the minimum tax rate, the slope of the tax schedule, the range of experience rated tax rates, and the penalty tax rate for employers with negative fund balances). Their research included theoretical and empirical analyses of how the parameters of the tax schedule can be altered to reduce inefficiencies in the UI system, i.e., to increase the utility of at least one of the arguments in the utility function without lowering utility in either of the other arguments. Their empirical analysis was conducted using three distinct types of models to characterize the behavior of actual and hypothetical UI programs. Unfortunately, they did not find many examples of tax parameter changes that unambiguously increased utility in all three models.

Although the framework and methodology of this research is founded in the neoclassical constrained maximization paradigm used by most economists, there are three points to note. First, the mean and the variance of the trust fund balance each enter two different arguments in the utility function and with opposite signs. Thus, if a state changes its tax schedule in a way that reduces year-to-year changes in employer tax rates, the variance of the fund balance will rise and increase the probability of insolvency (lowering utility), but at the same time this change will also increase the UI program's degree of tax smoothing (raising utility). Because of these offsetting effects, it is not possible in most situations to know how a change in the mean or the variance of the fund balance affects utility. Second, their research focused primarily on parameters of the tax schedule. Less attention was given to behavioral relationships determining insured unemployment, average weekly benefits, and the taxable wage base. State laws can affect these variables as well as the parameters of the tax schedule. All are important for understanding the behavior of the average trust fund level and trust fund variability. Third, the empirical work was conducted using a data period that ended in 1977. Some aspects of state behavior have been changing since the mid-1970s, particularly an increased willingness to enact solvency legislation when the trust fund balance moves towards zero, and these changes need to be recognized if future trust fund behavior is to be accurately modeled.

Freiman (1980) developed a model based on aggregate UI program data and used it to examine both trust fund financing problems of the mid-1970s and possible future financing problems in the 1980s and 1990s. He fitted multiple regressions to annual time series data for the years 1948 to 1974 to obtain parameters for the model's equations, including the tax rate equation. The tax rate depended on the lagged tax rate, the lagged trust fund reserve ratio, and a UI loan ratio (total loans as a percent of taxable payrolls). When the model was then used to simulate the years 1975–1977, he found that the tax equation made substantial overpredictions so that the simulated volume of UI loans was much less than actual loan disbursements of the three years. Freiman concluded that a major reason for the large loan volume of 1975–1977 was the small response of UI taxes (both tax rate and tax base increases) to declining reserve balances of these years.

Freiman's analysis also emphasized how high inflation causes financing problems for UI programs. In many states maximum weekly benefits rise with inflation while the taxable wage base does not respond. This causes tax revenues to grow more slowly than benefit payments in periods of high inflation.[24]

He further used the model to conduct simulations of UI trust fund balances in the 1980s and 1990s. In each of his long-run simulations, the UI system eventually encountered problems of fund inadequacy, due largely to the fact that benefits grow automatically with inflation and productivity growth while the tax base lags behind. Occurrences of high unemployment and/or high inflation, however, caused the funding problems to arise sooner. Given the high unemployment and high inflation that the U.S. economy experienced in the early 1980s, the funding problem predicted by his simulations became real experiences for many states.

This analysis is useful both for showing how the funding problems of the mid-1970s arose and how UI was exposed to a repetition of these problems in the 1980s. Because it was an aggregative analysis, however, it could not provide guidance to individual states as to the level of reserves needed to avoid insolvency, and Freiman did not attempt to provide aggregate solvency guidelines. His analysis was most useful for showing the harmful consequences of having a dynamic (indexed) benefit structure coupled with a static (nonindexed) tax base.

An alternative to the 1.5 reserve ratio multiple for assessing trust fund adequacy was developed in the mid-1970s at the South Carolina Employment Security Commission (1976). Like the 1.5 multiple, the South Carolina analysis yields a solvency standard against which a state's current trust fund balance can be compared. The South Carolina standard is easily understood and it can be computed from data routinely collected in a state's UI program.

There are three essential ideas in the South Carolina analysis of fund adequacy. (1) A UI program should strive to have stable tax rates. If the excess of taxes over benefits in prosperous periods matches the deficit of recession years, the state can cover its costs without needing to have fluctuating tax rates. Stable tax rates cause the UI program to impart the maximum countercyclical stimulus to the economy. (2) The required level of reserves (termed maximum reserves in the South Carolina analysis) must be sufficient to cover all outlays that will occur over a business cycle. Required reserves are computed as the product of three factors: (i) business cycle duration (in years); (ii) the average annual cost rate (benefits as a percent of total payrolls) over the business cycle; and (iii) the state's exposure to UI costs (the highest level of total payrolls). (3) Fund adequacy is assessed by comparing the ratio of actual reserves to required (or maximum) reserves. If actual reserves equal or exceed required reserves the state knows it can pass through a recession without having to raise taxes.

Besides these three key elements there are certain other aspects of the South Carolina analysis to be noted. (1) They advocate a system of array allocation for assigning tax rates to individual employers. Under array allocation the cost experiences of individual employers are ranked relative to average experience, and employers are assigned to tax categories where each category contains a fixed percentage of overall taxable wages. Array allocation ensures that for a given schedule of tax rates the aggregate ratio of tax receipts to taxable payrolls is stable from one year to the next. (2) They advocate having a flexible (indexed) tax base. (3) They stress the need for periodic reevaluation of the factors that contribute to UI benefit costs. This is done to ensure that historic cost rates remain appropriate for the current period. (4) They recognize a tradeoff between the level of the fund balance and the stability of tax rates. A state may choose to maintain a lower average balance if it is willing to change rates during the business cycle, i.e., to increase rates following an economic downturn.

Questions can be raised regarding the reliability of the South Carolina procedures for estimating a state's reserve requirements. How long is the period for measuring the length of the business cycle? Do past cost experiences provide a reliable guide for assessing future costs? If a state experiences a longer and/or a deeper recession than in the past, its reserves may be inadequate even if they satisfy the level specified by the South Carolina guideline. Of course, the 1.5 reserve multiple would also give misleading signals as to reserve adequacy if a future recession were longer and/or deeper than past recessions.

To evaluate the South Carolina guideline relative to the 1.5 reserve multiple it is instructive to calculate the level of reserves deemed adequate under the two. In one analysis (South Carolina Employment Security Commission 1976, chapter III), they estimate that required reserves for June 30, 1975 were $254.9 million. This calculation was made as follows: (1) business cycle duration—4 years; (2) high cost rate for four consecutive years—1.08 percent (1955--1958); and (3) exposure (1974 total payrolls)—$5.9 billion. The actual fund balance at the end of June 1975 was $130.9 million or 51 percent of its required balance. Under the 1.5 reserve multiple calculation, the highest cost rate prior to 1975 was the rate in 1954 of 1.54 percent. Using the same $5.9 billion of total payrolls causes the target fund balance to be $136.3 million under the 1.5 reserve ratio multiple guideline.

Thus the South Carolina guideline yields much larger reserve requirements than does the 1.5 reserve ratio multiple. This is hardly surprising since the fund balance is to equal four years of benefits at a four-year average cost rate rather than 1.5 years of benefits at a 12-month, high-cost rate. It should also be obvious that the difference in the two target levels for fund balances will be proportionally larger in states that have less severe cyclical cost experiences. Since the states do not now come close to meeting the 1.5 multiple guideline, the South Carolina guideline is even less attainable. It seems unlikely that any state would implement the South Carolina guideline and actually maintain a fund balance equal to four years of benefit outlays.

Baskin and Hite (1977) produced a lengthy report on fund adequacy under a U.S. Labor Department contract. Of the report's four chapters (I-Historical Summary, II-The 1.5 Reserve Adequacy Rule, III-Alternative Reserve Adequacy Rules, and IV-Recommendations), the analysis of their chapter III is of most interest. Baskin and Hite investigated the relative effectiveness of four rules that could determine trust fund balances. Relative effectiveness was judged by the ability of each rule to prevent insolvency during recessions, i.e., borrowing because the trust fund was exhausted.

The study used a simulation methodology where annual data from individual states for the 1951–1976 period were the units of observation. Historic data on state tax collections and benefit payments were used and downturns were defined as periods (of one or more conservative years) when the trust fund balance declined.[25] During the 1951–75 period they identified a total of 365 downturns across all programs.

At the start of each downturn, the state's trust fund balance was set according to one of the following four rules: (1) the 1.5 reserve ratio multiple rule (where the high-cost base year was the highest-cost year actually experienced during the 1951–75 period); (2) the highest cost rate experienced for two consecutive years; (3) a reserve multiple rule where the multiple is the ratio of total covered wages to taxable wages in the preceding year (thus a multiple that rises between 1951 and 1975); and (4) a combination rule. The latter allows the state to choose the most favorable from among the prior three rules for preventing insolvency in each downturn.

All rules were quite effective in preventing insolvency, but clear differences were found in their relative effectiveness. Respectively, the number of insolvencies under the four rules were 33, 10, 32 and 8. The percentage range of these numbers of insolvencies was from a high of 9.0 percent under the 1.5 reserve multiple rule to a low of 2.2 percent under the combination rule. Probably the most striking finding is that all four rules seem to be effective in preventing the need for borrowing by individual states.

The actual usefulness of the Baskin-Hite study can be questioned due to four methodological shortcomings. (1) Because the high-cost year used was the highest one for the entire 1951–75 period, the simulations assume a degree of foresight that the states could not be assumed to have. States could not reasonably be expected to set their reserves at the start of, say, 1954 on the basis of future high costs to be experienced in 1975. (2) In a similar vein, the combination rule is not really available to the states since it is determined in an *ex post* manner by the simulations and not on the basis of earlier state experiences. (3) There is no allowance for the possible responsiveness of tax collections (and benefit payouts) to reductions in trust fund balances. The initial trust fund balances, annual tax receipts and annual benefit payments are all treated as exogenous variables in the simulations. Among the most crucial research questions in determining appropriate fund balances, however, is the degree to which tax collections and benefit payments are endogenous, i.e., responsive to reductions in fund balances. (4) When the four rules are carefully compared, they suggest one obvious conclusion. This conclusion is illustrated with data appearing in appendix IIIA of the Baskin-Hite report. The appendix shows the cost rates for the base cost years underlying the 1.5 reserve ratio multiples and the two year cost ratios for each state as used in the simulations. In 42 of 51 states the latter is larger than the former by a ratio of more than 1.5 which means that the two year cost rule gives larger initial reserves in 42 of 51 jurisdictions. It is hardly surprising that use of the two year cost ratio produces fewer insolvencies, i.e., 10 as opposed to 33. A short summary of the study would be: larger reserves are more effective than smaller reserves in preventing UI trust fund insolvencies.

In summary, several final comments can be offered about the earlier literature on UI trust fund adequacy. First there are five critical comments. (1) The literature has not produced a major alternative to the 1.5 reserve ratio multiple as a useful rule of thumb for assessing fund adequacy. (2) Although the existence of excessive fund balances is a theoretical possibility emphasized by Bowes, Brechling and Utgoff (1980), the record of large-scale and widespread borrowing by the states in the 1970s and 1980s makes it clear that the real problem has been one of inadequate reserves. (3) Maintaining adequate reserves is exclusively a state responsibility in the 1980s. Therefore an aggregative analysis such as Freiman's (1980) does not provide guidance at the level where fiscal responsibility now resides. For example, his analysis does not show by how much the individual states should have raised their taxes in the mid-1970s to avoid insolvency. (4) The South Carolina analysis provides needlessly conservative guidance on the target or required level of a state's fund balance. (5) The analysis of Baskin and Hite (1977) cannot readily be used by individual states because it incorporates information on future cost rates not known prior to specific downturns, and it completely ignores the response of UI taxes (and benefits) to reductions in the fund balance.

Two more positive observations are the following. (1) To help avoid insolvency problems, states should apply indexing symmetrically to the tax and benefit sides of their programs. If the maximum weekly benefit is indexed, then the tax base should also be indexed. This is stated explicitly by Freiman and it is advocated by the South Carolina analysis. (2) The South Carolina analysis is useful for emphasizing the total amount of benefit outlays that a state must finance over a complete business cycle. This recognition of both business cycle duration and average annual costs is not incorporated into the 1.5 reserve multiple solvency guideline.

Summary

This chapter has examined several aspects of the UI financing problem, including a review of the previous literature. From rough calculations based on 1989 year-end reserve ratio multiples and the 1980-87 borrowing experiences of the states (from table 2.2), it appears that many UI programs remain exposed to a substantial risk of insolvency even after the large-scale trust fund building of the 1983–89 period. This calculation underscores the importance of knowing how large individual UI program trust fund reserves should be in order to achieve a low risk of small-scale borrowing in the next recession.

With the advent of interest charges on U.S. Treasury loans extended to debtor jurisdictions since April 1982, UI programs are much more inclined to avoid long-term debt than they were in the 1970s and the early 1980s. Since trust fund reserves are not that large, increased reliance on pay-as-you-go financing strategies may be expected. Some of this may be automatic pay-as-you-go financing, but undoubtedly there will still be some need for discretionary tax and benefit adjustments as fund reserves decline towards zero in the next recession.

The literature on UI financing reviewed here was not as helpful as would be hoped since much of the empirical analysis was based on experiences from the 1970s and earlier when reserves were larger and U.S. Treasury loans were interest-free. One actuarial guideline, the 1.5 reserve ratio multiple rule, was examined, but achievement of reserve levels suggested by this guideline would require a 77 percent increase in total reserves as of the end of 1989 (from $36.9 billion to $65.4 billion). Given the experiences of the 1980s, it appears that many UI programs can function successfully with reserve balances considerably smaller than suggested by the 1.5 reserve multiple rule.

Thus, several questions related to UI trust fund adequacy remain. Among them, the following will be addressed in chapter 4. For reducing the risks of insolvency, how quantitatively important are the automatic pay-as-you-go tax and benefit features now found in many UI program statutes? How much would the introduction of tax base indexation reduce risks of insolvency in programs that presently index their maximum weekly benefit but not their taxable wage base? Are stock-based and flow-based experience rating systems equally prone to the risk of insolvency? What level of trust fund reserves is needed to reduce the risk of insolvency to only needing a small UI loan in a recession? Technical questions of this nature are addressed in chapter 4, applying a simulation methodology in seven large states.

NOTES

1. Sections of this chapter draw heavily upon a report completed in 1986 for the U.S. Department of Labor and published in 1987. See Barnow and Vroman (1987), chapters II and III.

2. Michigan and Pennsylvania use both reserve ratios and benefit ratios to set employer tax rates. They have been classified among the 20 benefit ratio systems in the present discussion. Thus the 32–20 split between stock-based and flow-based tax systems would be changed to a 34–18 split if the two states were reclassified.

3. At the level of individual employers, the practice of experience rating is also intended to encourage long-term job tenure and to discourage layoffs. This important micro objective of experience rating will not be emphasized in the present analyses.

4. See chapter 19 in Haber and Murray (1966), pp. 380-385, for a discussion of the early experiences of the states with solvency standards.

5. Data on interest income by state appear in U.S. Department of Labor (1983) and subsequent Handbook updates. Nominal interest rates were high in this period, above 8 percent in each year between 1980 and 1986.

6. Estimates of the number of UI programs with automatic tax and benefit features were made by the author based on National Foundation for Unemployment Compensation and Workers' Compensation (1988), tables 3, 12 and 18.

7. The three indicators are as follows. (1) The average effective tax rate on Illinois employers must be at least .2 percentage points above the national average. (2) The trust fund balance as of March 31st must be less than $250 million. (3) Initial claims for benefits must be at least 25 percent above the average for the previous five years. The maximum weekly benefit is frozen in years when two of these conditions are met and reduced by 10 percent when all three conditions are met.

8. Robert Malooly, the former Manager of UI Actuarial Services, Illinois Department of Employment Security, described the results of the Illinois simulations in a conversation with the author.

9. See the 1987 testimony of Ms. Sally A. Ward, Director of the Illinois Department of Employment Security, and the associated statement for the record in U.S. House of Representatives (1987), pp. 96-106.

10. Details of the 1982–83 tax changes in Louisiana and Texas are given in chapter 2 of Vroman (1986).

11. In many reserve ratio systems, the excess of negative balances beyond a certain threshold size is eliminated so that employers are never responsible for repaying these charges against their accounts.

12. See, for example, tables 2–5 and 2–6 in Vroman (1986).

13. See chapter 2 in Haber and Murray (1966).

14. Loans during 1972–79 were less than 1 percent of 1975 covered payrolls in the following nine states: Alabama, Arkansas, Florida, Maryland, Montana, Nevada, New York, Ohio, and Oregon.

15. Loans during 1980–87 were less than 1 percent of 1984 covered payrolls in 18 programs: Alabama, Connecticut, Delaware, the District of Columbia, Indiana, Maine, Missouri, Montana, New Jersey, Rhode Island, South Carolina, Tennessee, Utah, Vermont, Virginia, the Virgin Islands, Washington, and Wyoming.

16. The 53 programs in the two periods give a total exposure of 106 programs compared to a total of 27 programs that needed small loans. Thus the average probability of a UI program receiving a small loan in the 1970s and 1980s was .255.

17. Total covered wages of taxable employers in 1975 and 1984 were respectively $580 billion and $1369 billion. The estimates of $.7 billion and $1.7 billion in loans were made by taking .5 percent of one-fourth (the assumed probability of insolvency) of these two covered wages totals.

18. The 12 were Connecticut, Delaware, the District of Columbia, Illinois, Michigan, Minnesota, New Jersey, Pennsylvania, Puerto Rico, Rhode Island, the Virgin Islands, and Vermont.

19. The 11 were Arkansas, Kentucky, Louisiana, Maine, Montana, North Dakota, Ohio, Texas, Washington, Wisconsin, and West Virginia.

20. See chapter 3 in Vroman (1986).

21. Having indexed their taxable wage bases prior to the onset of recession has helped many states to avoid large-scale borrowing or to completely avoid borrowing.

22. The $1-3 billion range is based on the same kind of calculations as described previously in footnote 16, but recognizing random elements in the number of states needing small loans, the average size of their covered payrolls, and the average size of their small loans.

23. The 15 states that were major borrowers in the 1974-79 period borrowed a total of $5.0 billion. The 14 that were major borrowers in 1980-87 received $23.2 billion in loans. These amounts represented 2.7 percent and 4.7 percent of their respective 1975 and 1984 payrolls.

24. In 1988 there were 17 UI programs whose maximum weekly benefit was indexed to average wages but whose taxable wage base was not indexed.

25. Primary and secondary downturns were distinguished. The start of the latter can follow the end of the former by as little as one year during which the trust fund increased in size. There were a total of 208 primary downturns and 157 secondary downturns.

3
A New Model
of Unemployment Insurance
Trust Fund Balances

Questions about UI trust fund reserve adequacy can be fruitfully studied within the framework provided by an economic model. The present chapter introduces and describes UISIM, a simulation model developed specifically to examine solvency issues. The next two chapters then use the model, as developed in several states, to make inferences about trust fund reserve adequacy.

Simulation Modeling With LOTUS

This section discusses how LOTUS spreadsheets can be used to examine UI funding questions. As a starting point, it reviews other simulation modeling efforts that have been fostered by the U.S. Department of Labor.

The most widely used model for addressing UI funding questions is the State Benefit Financing Simulation Model (SBFSM) originally developed for the U.S. Department of Labor by Mercer Associates (1977). The SBFSM, which continues to be supported by the Labor Department's Unemployment Insurance Service (UIS), is a very large scale model using quarterly data to simulate alternative trust fund scenarios for 10-year periods. To date, the SBFSM has been implemented in more than half of the states.

The model has two main sections: the Projection Program (PP) and the Financial Forecast Program (FFP). The PP section determines the important labor market variables for the state's economy and the various economic and statutory factors that affect UI benefit payments. The FFP section then combines output from the PP section with equations that characterize the state's UI tax statutes and the distribution of employers by tax rate categories to determine tax receipts. Simulations with the full SBFSM determine benefits, taxes and the state's trust fund balance for the period of interest.

The SBFSM is the most complete UI modeling capability available at the present time. Nevertheless, certain features of the SBFSM make it less usable than is desirable for some applications. The model is very large and its programming language is sufficiently imposing to discourage user-initiated changes in individual behavioral relations. Because the model is so large, it requires a major effort to reset the exogenous variables whenever a new, i.e., more recent, base period is to be used. Finally, recent advances in computer software capabilities, e.g., the LOTUS spreadsheet, provide an alternative approach for simulation modeling.

Many UI financing questions can be addressed with a much smaller model than the full SBFSM. One impetus for developing a smaller model was provided by a recent project on UI trust fund adequacy. In research supported by the U.S. Department of Labor, a small-scale annual model was developed to address funding issues. (See chapter IV in Barnow and Vroman (1987).) That model, termed the Annual Simulation Model or ASM, had very few equations and was imbedded within a Fortran program. Subsequent work with LOTUS spreadsheets led to the development of a UI simulation model based on LOTUS.

The model to be described, UISIM, is an annual model composed of from seventy to one hundred equations per state. It can be implemented without the need for Fortran programming, compiling, or the other steps usually followed in simulation and forecasting exercises. The model is structured as a rectangular grid of cells, with variables in the rows and time periods (years) in the columns. Each cell will contain a behavioral relation, a definitional identity, or the numeric value of a variable if it is exogenous to the model. Parameter values for the behavioral relations in UISIM are estimated using time series regressions with data from sources such as *Unemployment Insurance Financial Data* and "Significant Provisions of State Unemployment Insurance

Laws" published by UIS, *Employment and Earnings,* and the "Geographic Profile of Employment and Unemployment" published by BLS, or specialized data from the states themselves.

For the present project, simulation models were developed in seven large states: California, Florida, Massachusetts, Michigan, New Jersey, Ohio, and Texas. Because the states are widely distributed across the U.S., they encompass a variety of regional economic experiences. They are also representative of the most common experience rating systems: four use reserve ratios (California, Massachusetts, New Jersey, and Ohio); two use benefit ratios (Florida and Texas); and the seventh (Michigan) uses both reserve ratios and benefit ratios. (Experience rating systems as incorporated into the simulation models are discussed more fully in the next section of this chapter.)

It should be noted that UISIM produces deterministic solution paths for all variables. As presently implemented, there are no stochastic (i.e., random) elements that may vary from one simulation to the next imbedded in either the coefficients of the behavioral equations or their disturbance terms. Thus UISIM is like the SBFSM in that two simulation runs based on identical time paths for the exogenous variables and identical behavioral equations will yield identical solution paths. Random elements in the coefficients and/or disturbance terms could be added as inputs, but this type of extension of UISIM has not yet been explored.

Because UISIM has been developed for use on the types of spreadsheet programs available from the LOTUS Development Corporation (or comparable spreadsheet programs) a brief discussion of this software may be useful for some readers. LOTUS spreadsheets have a wide variety of uses on microcomputers. (See LeBlond and Cobb 1985.) LOTUS is designed to compute solutions to systems of equations where there is a clear sequential ordering for the effects of individual variables on other variables. In the jargon of economic model builders, LOTUS solves recursive (as opposed to simultaneous) equation systems.

The stocks and flows in state UI programs are appropriately modeled within a recursive framework. At the start of this year, the trust fund balance and employer tax rates are known. Consequently, the change in the fund balance during the current year depends primarily on variables that influence the outflow of benefit payments. Variables from this year (and perhaps previous years) determine next year's taxes. Thus there is a clear sequential ordering of causal relations within UI programs, i.e., a recursive ordering.

Probably the most powerful feature of LOTUS for simulation analysis is its automatic spreadsheet recomputation capability. A model is depicted as a rectangular array in the spreadsheet; each column represents a year and each row represents a particular variable in UISIM. When one exogenous variable is altered (for one year or a series of years), the effects of the change on all other variables in all years of the simulation period are computed automatically and displayed on a revised spreadsheet. There is no need to call a recomputation command because automatic recomputation is built into LOTUS. For example, the user can increase the state's overall unemployment rate (or TUR) by 1 percentage point in a single year. The effects on all variables in that year are computed, and (because of lags in individual equations and the trust fund identity) the effects in all subsequent years are computed as well. It is difficult to imagine how easily sensitivity analysis can be performed when automatic recomputation is built into the model.

Three other LOTUS features also facilitate simulation modeling. First, recall that an individual cell in a worksheet can be a number, an identity, or a behavioral equation. After an equation has been entered into one cell, the equation can be copied into all other cells, i.e., years, for that row. Thus a behavioral relation can be applied in all years with just its entry into one cell and use of the copy command. This feature makes it easy to explore the effects of changing a single behavioral relationship in the model. If, for example, the effect of indexing the tax base is of interest, an equation linking the tax base to the lagged average weekly wage can replace an existing tax base series which is exogenously determined (as it is in most states).

Second, one can use a variety of logical functions in the individual cells. Examples of "if" statements are: extended benefits (EB) are turned "on" only if the insured unemployment rate (IUR) exceeds a statutory threshold; interest accrues to the trust fund only if the average trust fund balance is positive and an indexed weekly benefit maximum can be frozen at its present level if the net trust fund balance is negative. The "round" statement can be used to replicate actual statutory language, e.g., in New Jersey the taxable wage base is rounded to the nearest $100 multiple of 28 times the average weekly wage; or a tax rate can be rounded to the nearest .01 percent; or the maximum weekly benefit can be rounded to the nearest whole dollar. Rounding up or rounding down can also be accomplished with the appropriate addition or subtraction of a constant within the "round" statement. The "maximum" and "minimum" functions can be used to ensure that the maximum tax rate and minimum tax rate cannot exceed their statutory limits.

LOTUS also permits the model builder to specify nested logic statements within individual cells. For example, if the raw calculation of the noncharged benefits tax rate exceeds zero (as in Michigan), the tax rate is the minimum of the calculated rate or 1 percent. Here, the "if" conditional (the raw tax rate exceeding zero) is followed by a "then" calculation which itself involves a logical comparison (selecting the smaller of two possible tax rates). An extension of nested logic statements to "macros" is also possible.

Third, LOTUS has a split screen feature which allows the user to focus on one area of the spreadsheet, e.g., the trust fund balance, while retaining the ability to scroll to and view other parts of the spreadsheet, e.g., a particular exogenous variable such as the state's total unemployment rate (TUR). The split screen capability is particularly convenient in a sensitivity analysis where the user wants to explore the effects of one exogenous variable on just one or a few other variables without looking at model output for all variables. All of these LOTUS features have been adopted in the development of the simulation models used in this project.

A General Description of UISIM

The spreadsheet models for each of the states share a number of common features. The following paragraphs first provide a general description of their structure and then a more detailed description for one state: Massachusetts. Each model has five main blocks of equations, and, as noted previously, each model is recursive.

Figure 3.1 helps provide an overview of the common features of the models. The figure identifies the five main blocks of equations. Also shown are the most important predetermined and exogenous variables within each block. These variables affect UI benefits, UI taxes, trust fund interest and the end-of-year fund balance. Variables from the UI system, however, do not feed-back on (influence) the predetermined and exogenous variables. The final column of figure 3.1 shows the most important simulation instruments. The response of the UI system to these simulation instruments is the main topic of the analysis in chapter 4.

The primary state labor market variables that affect UI taxes and benefits are determined in Block 1. These variables, which are treated as exogenous in the model, include the total unemployment rate, the inflation rate, the interest rate on UI trust fund balances, and the labor force growth rate. Labor force growth can reflect both national and state developments, but in the models used here no attempt was made to examine the determinants of state population growth or of state labor force participation rates. Labor force participation rates, for example, often decline in recessions, but the size of the decline is small and would not cause the models to make large errors. Inflation enters the model through the rate of change of average weekly wages. The total unemployment rate (TUR) is the most important exogenous variable because it ultimately drives the volume of claims for UI benefits. State-level projections of the important exogenous labor market variables may be obtained from state LMI (labor market information) offices or from forecasting services such as Data Resources Inc. and Wharton Econometric Forecasting Associates. Alternatively, the economic assumptions used by the state's budget office for intermediate-term budget projections can be imposed on the exogenous variables. In the simulation analysis of chapters 4 and 5, heavy reliance was placed on the past histories of state labor market variables from the 1970s and 1980s.

Important employment variables are also determined in Block 1. Total civilian employment is determined as a residual after the TUR and labor force growth rate have been set. Although both taxable and reimbursable employment covered by the UI program are influenced by state statutes, changes in both respond primarily to changes in total employ-

Figure 3.1
Outline of Unemployment Insurance
Simulation Model (UISIM)
A Recursive Model for the Evaluation
of State UI Trust Fund Financing[a]

Block	Predetermined and exogenous variables	Simulation instruments
1. Labor Market	Labor Force Growth Rate Total Unemployment Rate Wage Growth Rate	Total Unemployment Rate
2. Annual State UI Benefit Payments	Lagged Unemployment	Total Unemployment Rate Benefit Availability[b] Wage Growth Rate Maximum Weekly Benefit
3. Annual State UI Tax Receipts	Covered Wages State UI Tax Statutes	Regular UI Taxes UI Solvency Taxes Taxable Wage Base
4. Trust Fund Interest Income	Real Interest Rate	Real Interest Rate
5. State UI Trust Fund Balance	Start-of-year Fund Balance	Start-of-year Fund Balance

a. In this five block recursive simulation model the values of variables are determined by block in order. After values of the variables in the first block are determined, they feed into block two and so on.

b. Eligibility criteria for UI benefits were significantly tightened in all seven simulation states in the early 1980s.

ment and changes in national UI coverage provisions, e.g., the coverage extensions of 1972 and 1978. Therefore, the covered employment variables are also determined in Block 1 of UISIM.

Block 2 determines annual benefit payments, both in regular UI and the federal-state Extended Benefits (EB) program. The key variable in this block is insured unemployment (IU). Since 1980, the ratio of IU to total unemployment (TU) has fallen in most states. The explanation for this decline is not very well understood, but factors such as changes in statutory eligibility provisions, program administration, changes in the geographic distribution of unemployment, exhaustions by claimants, and application behavior have probably all contributed to the decline. (See the discussion in chapter 2 and the analysis by Corson and Nicholson 1988 and Burtless and Sax 1984, as well as Burtless 1983, Burtless and Vroman 1984 and Vroman 1990). The determination of insured unemployment is generally done in a similar way in the individual states. The three main explanatory variables are current unemployment (TU), a control for exhaustions (TU lagged one year) and a dummy variable for changes in program eligibility and participation in the 1980s.

Payments of regular UI benefits also depend on the weekly benefit amount and the ratio of weeks compensated to weeks claimed (52 times IU). The latter ratio is influenced by benefit statutes, e.g., the waiting period, maximum duration provisions and/or the length of benefit disqualification periods, and possibly by cyclical factors. The weekly benefit amount (WBA) depends on the average weekly wage, the maximum weekly benefit, and the statutory replacement rate. In most states, the maximum weekly benefit has changed much more than the statutory replacement rate, so that the estimated effect of the replacement rate on weekly benefits is not known.

States are also responsible for half of the costs of the EB program. Since EB is activated by the insured unemployment rate or IUR, i.e., the ratio of IU to total covered employment, and since the EB triggers are now different (higher) than in the 1971–1981 period, it is not obvious how EB should be modeled. One approach is to model the "on" trigger as a zero-one variable which equals one only when the IUR equals or exceeds a predetermined threshold. Weeks of EB could also depend on the IUR, perhaps with a lag. The weekly benefit amount (WBA) for EB would be expected to be similar to the WBA in the regular program. Half of EB payments along with all of regular UI benefits would then account for the outflow of benefits from the trust fund. Since the EB triggers are now higher than in the 1970s, and since the IU/TU ratio is now lower, the EB program is much harder to activate than in the past. Only six jurisdictions activated, i.e., turned on, EB between the end of 1982 and the end of 1988 (Alaska, Idaho, Louisiana, Puerto Rico, West Virginia, and Wyoming). The models can provide indications of how much EB would be paid under present EB triggers and under the (lower) triggers of the 1970s.

Total tax payments are determined in Block 3 as the product of total covered wages, the taxable wage proportion and the effective tax rate on taxable wages. Total covered wages are known from variables determined in Block 1, i.e., covered employment of taxable employers and the average weekly wage. The taxable wage proportion depends mainly on the ratio of the taxable wage base (an exogenous variable in most states) to average annual wages, i.e., 52 times average weekly wages. The functional form of this relationship is nonlinear. As the tax base-to-average wage ratio increases, so does the taxable wage proportion, but at a decreasing rate. The curvature in the relationship can be approximated by a second degree (or higher order) polynomial.

The determination of the effective tax rate on taxable wages is modeled in different ways in the individual states, a reflection of the major differences in their individual tax statutes. A fundamental distinction involves the type of experience rating present in the state. Nearly all states use either a reserve ratio approach or a benefit ratio approach to set tax rates for individual employers. Benefit ratio systems rely heavily on the flow of benefit payments (over the past, say, three years) relative to covered payroll in determining tax rates. Reserve ratio systems rely mainly on the ratio of the employer's trust fund balance to covered payroll to determine employer rates.

In reserve ratio states, the determination of the effective tax rate is modeled as a two step process. Most reserve ratio states have a tax code that provides for several different schedules of statutory rates. Experience rating provisions determine which schedule is in effect in any given year.

Higher tax schedules apply after a state has had bad experience (as indicated by a low trust fund balance). In reserve ratio states, the model uses a measure of experience to activate the appropriate tax schedule. Statutory rates from that schedule along with a measure of the overall reserve ratio (reserves as a percent of covered wages) are primary determinants of the effective tax rate.

In benefit ratio states, the aggregate benefit ratio (benefits as a percent of covered payroll) for the appropriate recent period is the main determinant of effective tax rates. Minimum statutory tax rates may also be important to finance benefit payments that cannot be assigned to individual employers (so called noncharges, ineffective charges and charges against inactive employer accounts).

Block 4 determines interest payments as the product of an exogenously determined interest rate and the average fund balance for the year. Block 5 contains the elements of the state's trust fund identity. The sum of taxes plus interest minus benefits is added to last year's balance to arrive at this year's balance.

To anyone who has worked with UI models, there are few surprises in UISIM as just described. The model described here is an annual model, but there is nothing that precludes the construction of a quarterly model. A quarterly model would have more equations and would have to explicitly address issues of seasonality. The emphasis on TU as well as IU as an important unemployment variable reflects my belief that TU is the more basic of the two unemployment measures. A version of UISIM could be built which used only IU, and many state practitioners might be inclined to do this.

A simulation model to analyze fund solvency has to determine benefits, taxes and interest income separately, cumulate these flows and update the fund balance periodically in order to track the trust fund over the period of study. What is new with UISIM is the way it is implemented using LOTUS. The model's equations are entered directly into a spreadsheet where the needed simulation calculations are performed automatically. There is no need to code and compile an elaborate computer program containing the model's equations. In short, UISIM is much more user-friendly than an earlier generation model like the SBFSM.

A Model of Massachusetts

During 1987 and 1988, the General Accounting Office conducted a review of state unemployment insurance programs that included an analysis of solvency questions. (See U.S. General Accounting Office 1988.) As one part of the solvency analysis, they requested that a simulation model be built to examine the effects of alternative macro scenarios on fund adequacy. Since many states are acknowledged to have inadequate balances, it was decided to study a state with a "large" balance to see if the balance would prove adequate in the face of a serious recession. Massachusetts was selected and became the first state where UISIM was implemented. (See Vroman 1987.)

On December 31, 1986, Massachusetts had a fund balance of about $1.0 billion, the sixth largest in the UI system. The state's reserve ratio (reserves as a percent of covered wages) of 2.0 percent ranked 16th highest among the 53 U.S. programs. At the end of 1987, reserves were almost $1.1 billion and the reserve ratio was again 2.0 percent. Thus, on both an absolute and a relative basis Massachusetts has had a large trust fund in recent years.

The growth of high-tech employment and military procurement in the 1980s have helped the Massachusetts economy to grow rapidly and reduce its unemployment rate to less than 4 percent. Massachusetts has an interesting history of cyclical experiences. It prospered in the late 1960s, but then had consistently high unemployment throughout the 1970s. Its unemployment rate (TUR) peaked at 11.2 percent in 1975, 2.7 percentage points above the national rate of 8.5 percent. The UI program in the state experienced funding problems in these years. Despite high tax rate levies, the fund balance was depleted, and the state borrowed $265 million during 1975–1976. Since then the state's unemployment rate has fallen, both absolutely and relative to the national average. In 1986 the state's unemployment rate was 3.8 percent whereas the national unemployment rate was 7.0 percent and in 1987 the corresponding state and national unemployment rates were 3.2 percent and 6.2 percent respectively. In summary, the state experienced an above-average TUR from 1971 to 1977, an average TUR in 1978, and a below-average TUR in all subsequent years.

The model of UI in Massachusetts has 76 equations. Each equation appears in appendix A, along with definitions of all the variables. Behavioral equations were first estimated for the period 1967–1985 or 1967–1986, but later the estimation period was extended to 1967–1987. Although the model was first implemented in simulations for the U.S. General Accounting Office (1988) that covered the years 1987–1996, it has been updated to examine the 1988–1997 period in the present analysis. Because the procedures for modifying equations and updating individual data series are straightforward in LOTUS, the updating of UISIM in Massachusetts was completed in about two days. The ease of updating is a convenient feature of LOTUS-based simulation models.

Of the exogenous labor market variables in Block 1, the labor force is assumed to grow at a rate that is three-fourths of the national growth rate for the 1987–1995 period as projected by BLS. (See Fullerton 1985.) This assumption was based on a comparison of state and national labor force growth rates for two periods; 1970–1975 and 1980–1985. Since very high unemployment prevailed during 1975–1980, these years were not used in the Massachusetts-U.S. comparison. The other main exogenous variables (the growth in weekly wages, the interest rate, and the TUR) can assume any values needed for a specific investigation. Of particular interest would be a repetition of the state's high unemployment of the 1970s.

Total state employment is known once the labor force growth rate and the TUR have been set. Total employment, in turn, is the primary determinant of taxable covered employment. The regression coefficient for total state employment was almost exactly 1.0 in an equation explaining taxable employment that covered the years 1967–1987 and included controls for the coverage expansion of 1978 and the rapid employment growth of 1985-1987. After examining residuals from the regression, however, it was decided to correct for first order serial correlation. This modification of the estimating equation reduced the large positive residuals that had been present at the end of the data period. For the model, the intercept in this equation has also been adjusted to correct for serial correlation in the residuals.

Reimbursable employment has grown rapidly over the 1972-1987 period, with the largest increase occurring in 1978 when coverage was expanded. The effects of Proposition 2 1/2 (a state tax initiative that placed a cap on property tax rates) and cutbacks in public service employment under CETA in 1981 and 1982 were also obvious as reimbursable employment fell sharply in these two years. In the model, reimbursable employment is assumed to increase by five for every one hundred increase in taxable employment above its 1987 level.

Insured unemployment (IU) is the most volatile of the endogenous variables determined in Block 2. In Massachusetts, 94 percent of the variation in IU between 1967 and 1987 was explained by a regression equation that used as explanatory variables TU, TU lagged one year, and a dummy variable which equaled 1 from 1981 to 1987. The respective unemployment coefficients were .533 and -.207 on TU and TU lagged, and both were highly significant. Lagged TU is apparently capturing the effects of exhaustions. The dummy variable for the 1981-1987 period was also found to have a significant negative coefficient suggesting a downward shift in IU in the 1980s. The size of the shift coefficient (-7,302) represented a 9.1 percent reduction in IU during the 1981-1987 period. In other regressions to explain the IU/TU ratio in Massachusetts, the shift dummy's coefficient was of a similar size (suggesting roughly a 10 percentage point reduction) and highly significant. Even in this state, which has enjoyed a high level of economic prosperity in the 1980s, a reduced fraction of the unemployed have been receiving UI benefits since 1981.

The gross replacement rate (the ratio of average weekly benefits to average weekly wages) was essentially trendless in Massachusetts from 1967 to 1986 as its main statutory determinants did not change. The maximum weekly benefit (as a percent of average weekly wages), the statutory replacement rate, and the size of dependents' allowances were all stable. In a multiple regression covering the 1967-1987 period, however, both the unemployment rate and the growth rate in average weekly wages were significant in explaining short-run variation in the gross replacement rate. A dummy variable for just the 1985-1987 period also was positive and significant. Higher unemployment raises the replacement rate as more senior workers enter the claimant pool during recessions. Greater wage inflation lowers the replacement rate as benefits are based largely on last year's wages, but the replacement rate is calculated on this year's wages. It is not clear what effect is being proxied by the 1985–1987 dummy variable.

Average weekly benefits are determined as the product of the replacement rate and average weekly wages. Massachusetts raised its dependents' allowance from $6 per dependent to $15 in 1987 and to $25 in 1988, but continued to limit the total dependents' allowance to half of the worker's average weekly benefit. In recognition of the increased payment per dependent, the average weekly benefit was raised by $5 in 1987 and by $8 in 1988 and later years (amounts suggested by a UI official in Massachusetts).

Besides IU and average weekly benefits, the other variables that determine total payments of regular UI benefits are: (1) the ratio of IU among taxable employers to total IU (including reimbursable employers); (2) the ratio of weeks compensated to weeks claimed; and (3) a final benefit adjustment ratio. After examining each of these variables it was decided to treat all three as exogenous, and to set each one to its average value for the 1983–1987 period.

The determination of extended benefits (EB) payments starts with the EB triggering mechanism. If the state's insured unemployment rate (IUR) averages 5 percent for any 13-week period, and the IUR is at least 20 percent above the average IUR for the same 13-week period in the previous two years, this will activate the EB program. Examining quarterly IURs for the 1979–1985 period, it was found that the average seasonal factor in the IUR for the first calendar quarter was 1.257. This implies that an annual IUR of 3.98 percent would be expected to produce a first quarter IUR of 5 percent. Thus EB is triggered "on" when the IUR reaches 3.98 percent. Weeks of EB (measured as annualized weeks and expressed as a proportion of weeks of regular UI benefits) are then determined from a regression on the average of the IUR for the current year and the previous year. The number of months that EB is "on" then increases as the IUR increases. It starts at three months, and when the IUR reaches 5.6 percent, the program is "on" for all

12 months. The weekly benefit in EB is set at 90.9 percent of the weekly benefit in regular UI (the average ratio for the 1980–1982 period) After total EB payments have been estimated, half are assumed to be the state's share. Half of EB along with all regular UI payments account for the total annual benefit outflow from the trust fund.

Tax collections from taxable employers depend on the product of three variables: total covered wages, the taxable wage proportion, and the effective tax rate on taxable wages. Since its inception, the Massachusetts program has generally used the federal tax base as the state's tax base. The only exception occurred between 1962 and 1971 when the state's tax base of $3600 exceeded the federal tax base by $600. Assuming that the state continues to follow the federal tax base in the future, the time path of the taxable wage proportion will depend mainly on the rate of wage inflation. In the model, the taxable wage proportion depends on the ratio of the taxable wage base to annual wages (52 times average weekly wages) and the TUR. The tax base-to-annual wages ratio enters as a homogeneous second degree polynomial, i.e., a polynomial with no intercept. This functional form ensures both that the relationship has curvature and that the taxable wage proportion goes to zero when the tax base-to-average wage ratio goes to zero. The regression explained 98 percent of the variation in the taxable wage proportion over the 1967–1987 period.

The Massachusetts statute provides for seven different tax schedules to be used in setting employer taxes. Statutory rates range from 1.2 to 5.4 percent of taxable wages under the most favorable schedule and from 3.0 to 7.2 percent under the highest schedule. The trust fund reserve ratio as of September 30th (reserves on that date as a percent of total covered wages for the preceding calendar year) determines which schedule will apply to taxable private employers in the next calendar year. In this calculation, Massachusetts allows the October tax payment (on average 13.4 percent of annual tax revenues) to be credited to employer reserves. A series of conditional (or if) statements are used in the model along with the September 30th reserve ratio to select the appropriate tax schedule for the next year.

Once the appropriate schedule has been identified, statutory rates from that schedule are used as a prime determinant of the average effective tax rate. In Massachusetts, the simple average of each tax schedule's minimum rate and maximum rate is used as a proxy variable to represent statutory rates from that schedule. This average is a key variable in a multiple regression to explain the average effective tax rate on taxable employers. Two other explanatory variables in the tax rate equation are a post-1978 dummy variable (to capture the effect of introducing a revised set of tax rate schedules in 1978) and the start-of-year trust fund reserve ratio (to capture movements along a given tax schedule). All three variables were highly significant in a regression that covered the 1967–1987 period, explaining over 98 percent of the variation in the effective tax rate.

Massachusetts also levies a solvency tax to replenish its solvency fund (a fund within the overall trust fund) each year. This fund is the source of payments for noncharged benefits and ineffectively charged benefits (benefit payments not charged to individual employers, benefit charges against active employers whose account balances are less than -15 percent of their taxable wages, and charges against inactive employers whose accounts have been exhausted.[1] The solvency fund received inflows from two sources: the state trust fund's interest income and solvency tax receipts. Prior to 1985, solvency taxes had been levied for several years at a flat rate of 1 percent on all taxable employers. Since 1985, the rate has been set to cover the excess of noncharges and ineffective charges over interest income. The solvency tax is a flat rate assessment levied at the start of the following calendar year. Rates of .05 percent and .07 percent were applied in 1986 and 1987 respectively.

In the model, the proportion of benefits that are noncharged and ineffectively charged is an inverse function of the state's start-of-year reserve ratio. The proportion ranges from .10, when the reserve ratio exceeds 4.0 percent, to a maximum of .27, when the reserve ratio is smaller than -.5 percent. After the solvency tax rate has been set, it is added to the regression-determined tax rate to yield the total effective tax rate on taxable employers. Total tax payments are then just the product of total covered wages, the taxable wage proportion and the total effective tax rate.

Blocks 4 and 5, which respectively determine interest income and the state trust fund balance, have no behavioral relations. Identities determine interest income and the trust fund balance. An if statement allows for interest income only if the average fund balance is positive. The interest rate is an exogenous variable linked to the rate of wage inflation. These blocks serve to close the model, but are of very little analytic interest. The economic variables, UI statutes and behavioral relations, that drive the model are found in the first three blocks of equations.

Models in Other States

Models similar to the Massachusetts model have also been developed in California, Florida, Michigan, New Jersey, Ohio, and Texas. All have a basic structure with five blocks of equations to respectively characterize each state's labor market, benefit payments, taxes, interest, and the trust fund identity.

The two behavioral equations that differ most across the seven states are the equations which determine taxable covered employment and the effective tax rate. Taxable covered employment in all states depends on total state employment (as measured in the monthly labor force survey). In several states there are also controls for the coverage extensions of 1972 and/or 1978. The equations differ in their use of employment variables from key industries. Three examples of key industry employment variables are as follows: construction employment in Florida, mining and manufacturing employment in Texas, and mining, manufacturing, and transportation employment in Michigan. Five of the seven models use a key industry employment variable, and they make highly significant contributions to explained variation in these states.

The effective tax rate equations have the most widely varying specifications across the states, a reflection of interstate differences in UI tax statutes. Typically, in reserve ratio states, a statutory tax rate and a measure of the state's overall reserve position are the principal arguments. The reserve ratio may measure the trust fund relative to either taxable wages or total wages depending on how the state's tax law is worded. In benefit ratio systems, the benefit ratio (benefits as a percent of covered payrolls) is always highly significant and measured over the time period stipulated by the state's law, e.g., in Texas the three years ending September 30th of last year. In some states, the tax rate equation also incorporates the provisions of a solvency tax designed to replenish the trust fund when it is drawn down to low levels.

Appendices B and C respectively provide full descriptions of the UISIM models as developed for Texas and Michigan. All variables are defined and all equations are shown in the same format as the description of the Massachusetts model given in appendix A. Combined, the three appendices provide examples of states with reserve ratio, benefit ratio and a hybrid reserve ratio-benefit ratio experience rating system.

The seven states are all large, and combined they accounted for 38 percent of taxable covered employment in 1987 (30.9 million workers out of a national total of 81.4 million). They represent a substantial share of aggregate UI program experiences. Because the seven are widely dispersed (two in each of the North East, the Midwest and the South and one in the West) their histories reflect regional as well as overall experiences with unemployment. Regional experiences are explored in chapter 5.

NOTE

1. The solvency tax in Massachusetts is not designed to increase total reserves of the state's overall UI trust fund.

4
A Simulation Analysis
of Fund Adequacy

This chapter uses UISIM as developed in seven states to examine questions about UI trust fund adequacy. Chapter 2 discussed in some detail three basic funding strategies that a state can follow. The state may prefund against future obligations by building a large trust fund balance, or it may plan to defray future benefit liabilities through an automatic pay-as-you-go strategy or a discretionary pay-as-you-go strategy. Under the later two strategies. fund balances may be restrained to lower average levels (vis-a-vis pre-funding), but taxes (and possibly benefits) respond more rapidly when recession-induced benefit outlays increase.

To help focus the analysis we will rely heavily on one operational indicator of funding inadequacy. The failure of a state to adequately finance its UI program will be inferred if the state's net trust fund balance is exhausted and the state requires "large" U.S. Treasury loans, i.e., total loans for an entire cyclical episode that exceed 1 percent of covered payroll as of one year (such as 1975 for the 1970s or 1984 for the 1980–87 period). This definition of what constitutes a large loan is admittedly arbitrary, but it permits a state to receive some loans without automatically concluding that its funding strategy is a failure. Since pay-as-you go strategies anticipate some borrowing, it is the need for large loans that signals a failure of the funding mechanism under this strategy.

Of the three funding strategies, the discretionary pay-as-you-go strategy is the least amenable to analysis through simulation modeling. This strategy contemplates legislative action to change tax statutes and/or benefit statutes to avoid insolvency. The need for discretionary changes is indicated by the (anticipated or actual) presence of trust fund debts, but the legislative response can take many forms when debts develop. The discretionary response arises within a legislative context that varies across states, something that does not fit easily within a simulation modeling framework.

81

What the simulation models can readily examine are the consequences for states of differing initial trust fund balances, the responsiveness of taxes (and perhaps benefits) under current UI statutes and the long-run implications for fund adequacy of current tax and benefit statutes. Thus the analysis of the models is most useful for assessing the pre-funding and automatic pay-as-you go strategies. These strategies can be examined because they presume that the present statutes of the UI system in a state remain unchanged. The statutes influence the way that UI taxes and benefits respond to changes in unemployment, inflation and other factors in the state's economic environment. What the simulation models can show are the need for discretionary changes and the size and the timing of needed changes if large scale borrowing is to be avoided. The borrowing needs of the states will be highlighted in subsequent sections of the chapter.

The States

The seven states selected for analysis are all large (among the top ten in taxable covered employment and covered wages and salaries), and combined they accounted for nearly 40 percent of covered U.S. employment in 1987. Besides their large average size, however, the states are diverse in a number of ways.

Table 4.1 presents summary information on several aspects of the states' diversity. The seven states are widely dispersed geographically, and they have had a variety of experiences with UI loans and debt in the 1970s and 1980s. Only California avoided borrowing altogether, while Michigan was the only large borrower in both decades.[1] The other five exhibit varying combinations of no loans, small loans and large loans in the two decades. There is a clear pattern of coastal states requiring large loans in the 1970s while interior states were more apt to be large borrowers in the 1980s. The geographic aspect of experiences with debt will be examined in some detail in chapter 5.

The seven states have a variety of experience rating systems. Four use reserve ratios and two use benefit ratios, while Michigan uses both

Table 4.1
Summary Information for the Seven States in the Simulation Analysis

State	Geographic region	UI loans in the 1970s[a]	UI loans in the 1980s[a]	Type of experience rating	Solvency tax	Indexed maximum weekly benefit	Indexed taxable wage base
Massachusetts	North East	Large	No	Reserve ratio	No	Yes	No
New Jersey	North East	Large	Small	Reserve ratio	Yes	Yes	Yes
Michigan	Midwest	Large	Large	Reserve ratio-benefit ratio	Yes	Yes[b]	No
Ohio	Midwest	Small	Large	Reserve ratio	Yes	Yes[b]	No
Florida	South	Small	No	Benefit ratio	Yes	No	No
Texas	South	No	Large	Benefit ratio	Yes	Yes[b]	No
California	West	No	No	Reserve ratio	Yes	No	No

SOURCES: National Foundation for Unemployment Compensation and Workers' Compensation (1988), tables 3, 5, 12, and 18 and loan calculations made by the author.

a. Large loans in the 1970s, i.e., loans exceeded 1 percent of 1975 payroll. Large loans in the 1980s, i.e., loans exceeded 1 percent of 1984 payroll.

b. Maximum weekly benefit frozen for two or more years between 1983 and 1988.

reserve ratios and benefit ratios to set employer tax rates.[2] Six of the seven states, all but Massachusetts, have some kind of solvency tax. Thus as trust fund balances approach zero, most have some provision for raising taxes that operates (at least partially) independently from the regular tax rate-setting procedure followed under experience rating. In four states the solvency tax is a separately identifiable tax, while in California and New Jersey the solvency tax is an extension of the regular experience rating tax schedules to a top (highest) schedule of statutory tax rates. There is an obvious interest in knowing the effectiveness of these extra taxes in preventing insolvency and/or large-scale borrowing. They represent an important element of an automatic pay-as-you-go financing strategy.

The seven states also have varied provisions regarding the indexation of the maximum weekly benefit and the taxable wage base. Only New Jersey indexes both, while Florida and California index neither. These three states can be described as having a symmetric indexation treatment of taxes and benefits (either indexing both or indexing neither) while the other four provide for an indexed weekly benefit maximum but not for an indexed tax base.[3]

The seven states selected for analysis differ in other ways besides those summarized in table 4.1. The lag between the tax computation date and date when new employer tax rates are imposed is six months in Michigan, New Jersey, and Ohio and three months in Massachusetts and Texas. Parts of tax computation arrangements followed in both California and Florida use information through the end of the current year to set the new tax rates that become effective on January 1 of the next year, i.e., a zero lag.[4] Florida and Texas use three years of recent experience for measuring individual employer benefit ratios, while the benefit ratios in Michigan cover five-year periods.

Two potentially important automatic pay-as-you-go features are absent from all seven states. None of the seven has a provision to automatically raise the taxable wage base or a provision to automatically freeze (or reduce) the maximum weekly benefit when the trust fund balance falls to a low level. Thus, although the sample of states is diverse in many ways, it does not exhaust the full range of potentially important UI financing provisions.

The Analytic Approach

A simulation analysis can cover a wide range of investigations into the effects of different exogenous variables, different behavioral relations, and different UI statutory provisions. This chapter examines only a limited number of topics. At the outset, each state's UI statutes (as of 1988) are taken as given, and the simulated time path of the trust fund balance over the 10 years from 1988 to 1997 is traced. Attention is then focused on the performance of the current UI program in response to changes in five variables: (1) the unemployment rate, (2) the inflation rate, (3) restrictions in the availability of UI benefits in the 1980s, (4) the real interest rate, and (5) the initial trust fund balance (as of December 31, 1987). Note that four of the five, all but changes in UI benefit availability, are beyond the state's immediate control. Later, the effects of solvency taxes on trust fund balances are examined. Reserve ratio and benefit ratio experience rating systems are also briefly compared in the section on tax responsiveness.

Each simulation makes explicit assumptions about all five of the control variables listed in the preceding paragraph. Note that the first four are flow variables that must be specified for each year of a simulation. A few added comments about the control variables should also be made.

Unemployment is probably the control variable of greatest interest since it exerts a strong and direct influence on the volume of UI claims. In each state, four time paths of the total unemployment rate (TUR) were singled out for explicit attention: the state TUR in the 1970s (1970 to 1979), the state TUR in the 1980s to (1979 to 1988), the national TUR in the 1970s; and the national TUR in the 1980s. Use of historic TUR data limits what otherwise could be any number of conceivable time paths of unemployment in the simulations. Two logical questions for analysis which follow from the choice of TURs are: How would the UI program fare if the state were to undergo a repetition of earlier unemployment experiences? and How would the state fare if its unemployment rate matched the national average? The choice of the TUR as the fundamental unemployment variable permits one to distinguish the effects of variation in overall unemployment from the effects of variation in the accessibility of benefits (e.g., the ratio of weeks compensated to total weeks of unemployment) in determining benefit payouts within a state.

It should also be noted that most time paths of the state TURs, like the national TURs, peak in the middle years of the 10-year simulation intervals, so that trust funds are usually growing at the end of the simulations (both from the response of experience rated taxes to earlier claims activity and from declining claims activity). The analysis focuses on borrowing over the entire 10-year interval as well as final trust fund balances.

The control variable for inflation is the annual growth rate in average weekly wages. As with unemployment, historic data on wage inflation from the 1970s and 1980s are utilized. To further explore the effects of inflation on fund balances, inflation rates that exceed historic experiences are also utilized. Attention on the real interest rate is especially relevant in the 1980s, as real interest rates (the nominal interest rate less the rate of wage inflation) have been unusually high. To explore the effects of differing initial trust fund balances, we use actual balances at the end of 1987 and alternatives that reflect actuarial guidelines (such as the 1.5 reserve ratio multiple).

The simulations also explore the consequences for states of changes in benefit availability in the 1980s. This is done by making two modifications in the models. Decreased benefit availability in the regular UI programs is approximated by a dummy variable shift effect in the insured unemployment equation. The effects of the higher EB triggers are also incorporated in the models. Both restrictions on benefit availability can be reversed to make the benefit payout patterns more closely resemble those of the 1970s.

A problem was observed in some initial simulations with the taxable wage base and maximum weekly benefit in states where these variables were not indexed. The minimum taxable wage base permitted in a state is the base used for the Federal Unemployment Tax (FUT), presently $7,000 per worker. This was the actual 1988 (and 1989) tax base in three simulation states (Massachusetts, Florida, and California). If the tax base is assumed to remain unchanged over the 10-year 1988–1997 interval, taxable wages decline to only 15 to 20 percent of total wages by the end of the simulation period. To counteract what may be viewed as an unrealistically low taxable wage proportion, the FUT tax base was raised to $9,000 in 1991 and to $11,000 in 1995. In the two states where the maximum weekly benefit is not indexed, the following assumptions were also made. California was assumed to raise its present $166 maximum to $205 in 1991 and to $250 in 1993. Florida's 1989 maximum of $200 was raised to $250 in 1993. All of these assumptions were somewhat arbitrary, but they seemed less unrealistic than assuming unchanged tax bases and weekly benefit maxima over the entire 1988–1997 interval.

The Baseline Simulations

The starting point for the analysis was a baseline simulation in each state where the unemployment rate was stable at roughly the full employment unemployment rate[5] and wage inflation was stable at a moderate rate. Two purposes were served by the baseline simulations. First, they showed the level that the trust fund balance would attain in the intermediate run under generally favorable economic conditions, given the initial trust fund balance and the 1988 tax and benefit statutes operative in the state. Second, they provide a background against which the changes in benefits, interest, taxes and fund balances could be measured when the important control variables departed from their baseline levels.[6]

The assumptions for the control variables in the baseline simulations were as follows. (1) The unemployment rate was 5.5 percent of the labor force. In three states where the 1987 unemployment rate was more than a full percentage point above 5.5 percent (Michigan, Ohio, and Texas), the rate in 1988 and 1989 was assumed to decline by about 1 percentage point per year until 5.5. percent was achieved.[7] (2) The wage inflation rate was assumed to be 6 percent per year. This rate is consistent with historic experiences in UI programs.[8] (3) The real interest rate was assumed to be 1 percent per year (or a 7 percent nominal interest rate in the baseline). This real interest rate is less than the average for the 1980s, but greater than the average for the 1970s. (4) Benefit availability in the regular UI and EB programs was assumed to be the same as in the 1980s, i.e., a downward shift from the 1970s in regular UI and the applicability of the current (higher) EB triggers. (5) Initial trust fund balances were those as of the end of 1987.[9]

Table 4.2 displays summary information from the baseline simulations. So much information is generated by 10-year simulations of models containing 70 to 90 equations that only a small portion of model output is shown. The three flow variables (taxes, interest and benefits) are summed for the entire 10 years, while fund balances and other reserve indicators are shown for the start and end of the simulation period. Observe that the average unemployment rate (TUR) is slightly above 5.5 percent in three states, a reflection of the assumption that unemployment gradually declines to 5.5 percent in the initial years of the simulations.

To provide indicators of trends on the benefit and tax sides of the programs, the table shows starting year and ending year measures for the ratio of the maximum weekly benefit amount to average weekly wages and the taxable wage proportion. The former is stable in three of five states where the maximum weekly benefit is indexed (Massachusetts, New Jersey, and Michigan). It rises in Ohio, reflecting a recoupment between 1988 and 1993 of earlier losses associated with a freeze in maximum benefits over the 1983–1987 period. It rises in Texas, due to the operation of an indexation formula which causes the maximum benefit to rise faster than average weekly wages.[10] The ratios decline in the two states where the weekly maximum is not indexed, Florida and California, and where the models assume the maximum reaches $250 by 1997. The taxable wage proportion is stable in New Jersey, which has an indexed tax base, and in Massachusetts, Florida, and California, the three states where the 1988 base is $7,000 (and assumed to rise to $11,000 by 1997). In the other three states, (Michigan, Ohio, and Texas) the taxable wage proportion declines because the starting (1988) tax base exceeds $7,000 but only grows to $11,000 by the end of the simulation period. Thus, in two of the states

Table 4.2
Baseline Simulation Results

		Massachusetts	New Jersey	Michigan	Ohio	Florida	Texas	California
Total unemployment rate (TUR) (%)		5.5	5.5	5.7	5.6	5.5	5.8	5.5
Wage inflation rate (%)		6.0	6.0	6.0	6.0	6.0	6.0	6.0
Maximum WBA/ AWW ratio	1988	0.599	0.496	0.503	0.445	0.538	0.503	0.357
	1997	0.599	0.504	0.520	0.525	0.398	0.546	0.318
Taxable wage proportion	1988	0.345	0.447	0.370	0.364	0.398	0.369	0.317
	1997	0.323	0.432	0.256	0.298	0.372	0.300	0.292
Taxes	1988–1997	8,316	11,730	10,141	10,042	5,308	10,832	26,033
Interest	1988–1997	564	2,023	1,361	1,549	1,704	922	4,081
Benefits	1988–1997	8,918	11,305	8,657	8,016	5,109	9,262	25,396
Interest/total trust fund receipts		0.064	0.147	0.118	0.134	0.243	0.078	0.136
End of year trust fund	1987	1,097	1,824	26	214	1,745	−514	4,017
	1997	1,058	4,272	3,540	3,789	3,648	1,979	8,735
Reserve ratio (% of covered payroll)	1987	1.96	2.65	0.04	0.29	2.38	−0.48	1.79
	1997	0.99	3.16	2.55	2.53	2.12	0.72	1.77
Reserve ratio multiple	1987	0.61	0.80	0.01	0.09	1.29	−0.42	0.76
	1997	0.31	0.95	0.69	0.82	1.15	0.63	0.75

SOURCE: Simulations with UISIM. Taxes, interest, benefits and trust fund balances measured in millions of dollars.

(Ohio and Texas), the UI programs become more unbalanced over the 1988–1997 period because maximum benefits grow considerably faster than weekly wages while the taxable wage proportion declines.

When the 10-year flows of taxes, interest, and benefits are examined, one noticeable feature of the simulations is the importance of interest income in overall trust fund receipts. In five states, interest accounts for more than 10 percent of total receipts and for more than 20 percent in Florida. The 10-year flows of benefits and taxes are roughly equal in several states, so that trust fund accumulations are due mainly to interest income. Having a large average trust fund balance yields substantial interest income to several states.

Primary interest in table 4.2 centers on the behavior of the trust fund balance over the 10 years. In all states but Massachusetts, nominal reserves grow and the accumulations are especially large in Michigan, Ohio, and Texas, the states with low initial balances. When the starting and ending balances are measured as a percent of covered payroll (i.e., as reserve ratios), one observes that the reserve ratios remain roughly constant in New Jersey, Florida, and California. The reserve ratio declines by roughly half in Massachusetts, while ratios grow substantially in the three states with low initial balances. Thus, of the seven states, only Massachusetts experiences a measurable decline in its reserve ratio in the baseline simulations.

Finally, the bottom rows of table 4.2 display starting and ending reserve ratio multiples. No multiple is as large as 1.5, a recommended actuarial standard, and only Florida's multiples exceed 1.0. By 1997, however, six states have multiples of at least .6, and only Massachusetts has a lower multiple (at .31).

To summarize, trust fund balances grow substantially in six of the seven states in the baseline simulations. For the seven programs combined total net reserves increase from $8.4 billion to $27.0 billion over 10 years, or from 1.25 percent to 1.83 percent of covered payroll. Despite the favorable economic environment of the baseline and substantial trust fund accumulations, no state achieves a 1.5 reserve ratio multiple by the end of 1997, and only one (Florida) achieves a multiple that exceeds 1.0.

Alternative Unemployment Simulations

During most years in the 1970s and 1980s, the average unemployment rate for the nation exceeded 5.5 percent, averaging 6.2 percent from 1970 to 1979 and 7.3 percent from 1979 to 1988. For the seven states under investigation, the statewide averages over the same time periods also typically exceeded 5.5 percent.[11] To analyze the performance of the individual UI programs under differing unemployment environments, a series of simulations were conducted which differed from the baseline simulations only in the time paths of the unemployment rate (TUR). State and national TURs from the 1970s and 1980s (1979–1988) were used in these simulations. The need for UI loans and the scale of borrowing were the outcome variables of central interest.

It should be emphasized that these (and later) simulations are not offered as predictions of the volume of borrowing that would occur for given time paths of unemployment. A state whose fund balance was observed to decline could enact legislation to increase taxes and/or reduce benefits to prevent insolvency or to reduce the scale of borrowing. What the simulations are intended to show is the borrowing that would take place given the state's initial trust fund balance and given the state's 1988 tax and benefit statutes. Discretionary policy actions lie outside the scope of the simulations.

In chapter 1, it was observed that states that incurred interest-bearing debts after March 1982 tended to repay such debts very quickly. Some of the loans received were needed for seasonal and other short-run cash flow needs when fund balances are low. The debtor states were often observed to borrow and then repay part or all of the loan within the same year. Since the simulation models were developed as annual models, they do not capture these very short term borrowing needs. Consequently, the volume of loans as simulated by UISIM in states whose trust fund balances are low or negative will systematically understate the actual extent of borrowing undertaken by states in such situations. This understatement should be kept in mind in judging the volume of loans required under the various unemployment scenarios. We estimate the volume of "cash flow" loans to have been substantial in Michigan, Ohio, and Texas in the 1982–1987 period, roughly half of all interest-bearing loans received in these years.[12] Thus, we will infer that a state needs large scale loans if total simulated loans for the 1988–1997 period equal .5 percent of 1992 payroll. This will make the loan estimates in the simulations roughly comparable with historic data from the seven states covering the 1970s and 1980s (and noted in table 4.1).

Table 4.3 summarizes the alternative unemployment simulations. No state requires UI loans in the baseline. The average TURs during 1988-1997 and 1997 fund balances from the baseline are shown so that the reader can compare baseline values of these variables with their values under the differing unemployment scenarios. Applying 1970s state TURs, two states, Massachusetts and Michigan, need loans. Using a .5 percent criteria for large loans (total loans relative to 1992 payroll), Massachusetts and Michigan both need large loans, as they actually did in the 1970s. The third large borrower from the 1970s, New Jersey (see table 4.1), needs no loans under this simulation scenario.

When the states are subjected to a repetition of state TURs from the 1980s, Michigan and Ohio are identified as major borrowers while Texas is simulated to require only a small loan. Note that Michigan and Ohio have especially high average unemployment rates, the highest average TURs in table 4.3, and both states end the simulations with negative net trust fund balances. Massachusetts, New Jersey, and Florida actually end these simulations with higher net reserves than in the baseline simulations, a reflection of the effects of declining TURs towards the end of the simulation period.[13]

The third set of unemployment simulations suggests that a repetition of national TUR experiences from the 1970s in the individual states would not pose serious financing problems. Texas is the only state that requires loans, and its borrowing totals only .09 percent of 1992 payroll. In all reserve ratio states, the 1997 reserve balances are measurably lower than in the baseline. The differences range from about $250 million in Massachusetts to $1 billion or more in New Jersey, Michigan, Ohio, and California. The ending fund balance (*vis-a-vis* the baseline) is only $41 million lower in Florida, and it is $142 million higher in Texas.

Table 4.3
Simulations with Alternative Unemployment Rates

	Massachusetts	New Jersey	Michigan	Ohio	Florida	Texas	California
Baseline simulation							
Average TUR (%)	5.5	5.5	5.7	5.6	5.5	5.8	5.5
Loans – 1988-1997 ($)	0	0	0	0	0	0	0
Fund balance – 1997 ($)	1,058	4,272	3,540	3,789	3,648	1,979	8,735
State unemployment rates of the 1970s							
Average TUR (%)	7.2	7.2	7.9	6.1	6.5	4.8	7.9
Loans – 1988-1997 ($)	789	0	808	0	0	0	0
Loans/1992 payroll (%)	1.03	0.00	0.81	0.00	0.00	0.00	0.00
Fund balance – 1997 ($)	312	1,408	-359	2,539	3,547	2,108	6,435
State unemployment rates of the 1980s							
Average TUR (%)	5.1	6.3	10.8	8.8	6.4	6.7	7.3
Loans – 1988-1997 ($)	0	0	4,316	3,953	0	466	0
Loans/1992 payroll (%)	0.00	0.00	4.32	3.72	0.00	0.26	0.00
Fund balance – 1997 ($)	1,917	4,438	-2,210	-3,119	3,933	431	7,709
U.S. unemployment rates of the 1970s							
Average TUR (%)	6.2	6.2	6.2	6.2	6.2	6.2	6.2
Loans – 1988-1997 ($)	0	0	0	0	0	171	0
Loans/1992 payroll (%)	0.00	0.00	0.00	0.00	0.00	0.09	0.00
Fund balance – 1997 ($)	811	3,063	2,466	2,390	3,609	2,121	7,524
U.S. unemployment rates of the 1980s							
Average TUR (%)	7.3	7.3	7.3	7.3	7.3	7.3	7.3
Loans – 1988-1997 ($)	479	0	0	436	0	951	0
Loans/1992 payroll (%)	0.63	0.00	0.00	0.41	0.00	0.53	0.00
Fund balance – 1997 ($)	751	2,469	1,662	1,044	3,828	3,026	7,456

SOURCE: Simulations with UISIM. Loans and reserves measured in millions of dollars.

Since the latter two states both use benefit ratio experience rating, we note this contrast with reserve ratio states here and explore it further in later sections of the chapter.

The bottom panel in table 4.3 shows results when each state experiences the national TURs from the 1980s. Since the 1980s average TUR is higher than the average from the 1970s (7.3 percent versus 6.2 percent), these simulations show more of an effect on the need for loans and final year trust fund balances. Three states (Massachusetts, Ohio, and Texas) borrow a total of $1,866 million. Again observe that the closing trust fund balances remain high in the benefit ratio states (Florida and Texas), whereas they decline in the reserve ratio states (except for California). Comparing the loan activity from these simulations with the simulations using 1980s state TURs ($1,866 million versus $8,735 million), it seems clear that the concentrations of unusually high unemployment in a few states (Michigan and Ohio) is what causes the much larger volume of loans in the simulations that use 1980s state TURs.

Based on the results shown in table 4.3, four conclusions about the effects of higher unemployment are suggested. First, modest increases of .5 percent to 1.5 percent in the average TUR (above the baseline) do not lead to financing problems in all states. When the average TUR increased to 7.3 percent (the U.S. TUR of the 1980s), three states needed loans, and for each state the scale of borrowing was close to the threshold used in the simulations to distinguish large from small loans (.5 percent of 1992 payroll). Across the seven states, however, the combined loan total of $1,866 million represented only .18 percent of payroll. Even after doubling this total to include borrowing for cash flow needs, the resulting .36 percent of payroll is much smaller than the borrowing that did take place in the 1970s and 1980s. Borrowing by these seven states in the 1970s totaled .79 percent of 1975 payroll, and in the 1980s it totaled 1.89 percent of 1984 payroll. Thus, under a repetition of national TURs from the 1980s in each of the seven states, total simulated borrowing (as a percent of payroll) was only about one-fifth of actual borrowing by these states in the 1980s.

Second, major borrowing was observed in two states that experienced unusually high average unemployment in the 1980s. The two states were found in the same region, the Midwest. Regional aspects of UI financing will be examined more fully in chapter 5.

Third, initial trust fund balances have an important effect on the need for UI loans. The three states that did not borrow in any of the simulations reported in table 4.3, (New Jersey, Florida, and California) were the states with the highest reserve ratio multiples at the start of the simulations (.80, 1.29 and .76 respectively). Later in this chapter, the effects of high initial fund balances are explored further.

Fourth, the results displayed in table 4.3 suggest that benefit ratio experience rating may be more effective than reserve ratio experience rating in maintaining trust fund balances in the face of high unemployment. The ending trust fund balances in Florida and Texas were generally as high in the high unemployment simulations as in the baseline simulations. We will return to this issue later in the present chapter.

Alternative Inflation Simulations

Variation in the rate of inflation, like unemployment, is an element in the economic environment that is beyond a state's ability to control. Experiences from the 1980s provide a clear illustration of the amount of inflation variation that can occur within a short period. Annual wage inflation averaged almost 10 percent at the start of the decade, dropped to less than 5 percent in the 1983–1986 period, and then began to move upward towards the end of the decade.[14]

The consequences of differing inflation rates for UI financing are much less dramatic than the effects of differing unemployment rates. High inflation over several years may make a program more prone to insolvency, but high inflation *per se* will not cause insolvency. High inflation can contribute to a financing problem if a state indexes its weekly benefit maximum but does not similarly adjust its taxable wage base (through indexation or periodic discretionary adjustments).

In this section we examine the consequences of nonsymmetric adjustments of the maximum weekly benefit and the tax base in the face of varying rates of inflation. New Jersey (which indexes both) is like

Florida and California (which index neither) in providing symmetric treatment, while the other four states have asymmetric treatment (indexing the maximum weekly benefit but not the tax base).

Table 4.4 summarizes the results from five simulations in each state, the baseline and four others. In each simulation, the inflation rate varies while unemployment and all other control variables repeat their baseline values. Before examining the consequences for reserves it is useful to briefly discuss the wage inflation averages themselves. Compared to average state unemployment rates from the 1970s and 1980s, the average state inflation rates exhibit much less variation. Across the seven states, average inflation rates in the 1980s (1979 to 1988) ranged from 4.9 percent to 7.7 percent, whereas the average state TURs (table 4.3) ranged from 5.1 percent to 10.8 percent.[15]

Because the entire range of state wage inflation experiences from the last two decades seemed rather limited, i.e., from 4.9 percent (Ohio in the 1980s) to 7.7 percent (Massachusetts in the 1980s), simulations were also conducted based on higher inflation rate averages (of 8.0 and 10.0 percent). These were used not necessarily as realistic alternatives but to expand the range of inflation variation. They help to illustrate how asymmetric treatment of maximum benefits and the tax base can contribute to financing problems.

Since high inflation expands covered payroll, the more relevant solvency indicator in five of the seven states is not the absolute level of trust fund reserves but rather the reserve ratio (reserves as a percent of payroll). Both are shown in table 4.4 as of 1997, the final year of the simulations. In states that index their maximum weekly benefit, potential obligations to pay benefits rise proportionately as inflation increases. Therefore, to maintain an initial degree of solvency it is important that the reserve ratio not decline when inflation increases. In states which do not index their maximum weekly benefit, potential obligations to pay benefits may grow more slowly than the inflation rate. A judgment about maintenance of solvency in such states involves a comparison of the change (decline) in the reserve ratio with the change in a nominal benefits indicator (such as the ratio of maximum weekly benefits to average weekly wages) when higher inflation takes place. If the reserve

Table 4.4
Simulations with Alternative Inflation Rates

	Massachusetts	New Jersey	Michigan	Ohio	Florida	Texas	California
Baseline simulation							
Wage inflation rate (%)	6.0	6.0	6.0	6.0	6.0	6.0	6.0
Maximum WBA/AWW – 1997	0.599	0.504	0.520	0.525	0.398	0.546	0.318
Fund balance – 1997 ($)	1,058	4,272	3,540	3,789	3,648	1,979	8,735
Reserve ratio – 1997 (%)	0.99	3.16	2.55	2.53	2.12	0.72	1.77
State wage inflation rates of the 1970s							
Wage inflation rate (%)	6.3	6.6	7.0	6.6	6.0	7.5	5.6
Maximum WBA/AWW – 1997	0.594	0.491	0.510	0.510	0.400	0.537	0.329
Fund balance –1997 ($)	1,088	4,528	3,743	4,081	3,686	2,108	9,074
Reserve ratio – 1997 (%)	0.99	3.17	2.47	2.58	2.15	0.67	1.90
State wage inflation rates of the 1980s							
Wage inflation rate (%)	7.7	7.0	5.0	4.9	6.4	6.0	6.7
Maximum WBA/AWW – 1997	0.588	0.493	0.545	0.541	0.384	0.540	0.297
Fund balance – 1997 ($)	965	4,710	3,208	3,475	3,648	1,828	8,529
Reserve ratio – 1997 (%)	0.77	3.17	2.56	2.57	2.04	0.67	1.61
8 percent wage inflation rate							
Wage inflation rate (%)	8.0	8.0	8.0	8.0	8.0	8.0	8.0
Maximum WBA/AWW – 1997	0.588	0.486	0.506	0.511	0.330	0.551	0.264
Fund balance – 1997 ($)	892	4,987	3,407	3,814	4,063	1,945	8,735
Reserve ratio – 1997 (%)	0.69	3.05	2.04	2.11	1.96	0.58	1.46
10 percent wage inflation rate							
Wage inflation rate (%)	10.0	10.0	10.0	10.0	10.0	10.0	10.0
Maximum WBA/AWW – 1997	0.578	0.468	0.493	0.495	0.275	0.555	0.220
Fund balance – 1997 ($)	572	5,965	3,186	4,098	4,495	1,913	7,768
Reserve ratio – 1997 (%)	0.37	3.04	1.59	1.89	1.80	0.48	1.08

SOURCE: Simulations with UISIM. Reserves measured in millions of dollars.

ratio declines more rapidly than the benefit indicator, this signals a deterioration in the state's solvency position. For each simulation the reserve ratio and the ratio of maximum weekly benefits to average weekly wages (in 1997) appear in table 4.4.

It is clear in table 4.4 that higher inflation causes important losses in reserve adequacy in several states, with Massachusetts providing the most dramatic evidence. Its 1997 reserve ratio of .99 in the baseline declines to .77 with a repetition of state wage inflation from the 1980s (an average of 7.7 percent). Under 10 percent annual wage inflation, the 1997 reserve ratio declines to .37 or 37.4 percent of its level in the baseline. Michigan, Ohio, and Texas also exhibit large losses in reserve adequacy by 1997 as the inflation rate increases above the 6.0 percent average of the baseline. Under 10.0 percent average annual inflation, 1997 reserve ratios range from 62.4 percent to 74.7 percent of their corresponding 1997 reserve ratios in the baseline, e.g., 62.4 percent in Michigan which has a 1997 reserve ratio of 1.59 percent under 10 percent inflation versus 2.55 percent in the baseline.

New Jersey, which indexes both the maximum weekly benefit and the taxable wage base, is the only one of the seven states whose reserve ratio remains nearly constant in the face of increasing inflation. Its 1997 reserve ratio under 10 percent annual inflation (3.04 percent) is 96.2 percent of the 1997 reserve ratio in the baseline (3.16 percent). Note that in Florida and California, higher inflation also causes 1997 reserve ratios to decline (*vis-a-vis* the baseline). Generally the lower reserve ratios in these two states coincide with lower ratios of maximum weekly benefits to weekly wages, so that the declines *per se* do not signal a loss of reserve adequacy.[16]

None of the simulations with higher inflation rates resulted in insolvency for any state. The insolvency threat that high inflation poses is that high inflation by itself causes a loss of reserve adequacy (when indexation is not symmetrically applied to the tax and benefit sides of UI programs) and makes the effects of high unemployment more serious (because reserve ratios are depleted). Stagflation (the simultaneous presence of high inflation and high unemployment) will lead to larger solvency problems for such states than will a given level of high unemployment operating in an environment of low inflation.

Effects of Variation in Initial Trust Fund Balances

Raising a state's initial trust fund balance will reduce the risk of insolvency and the scale of borrowing in the event of high unemployment. Supporters of UI solvency standards base their arguments for standards on such debt avoidance outcomes. If all states had entered the 1980s with reserve ratio multiples of 1.5, the volume of state borrowing would clearly have been much smaller than the actual $24.0 billion that was borrowed between 1980 and 1987.

Any serious public policy discussion regarding the desirability of solvency standards would benefit from a simulation analysis of technical questions related to appropriate levels of reserve balances. What is the average decrease in borrowing associated with each successive $1 billion increase in initial reserves? Could most of the loan-avoidance advantages of higher reserves be realized if the initial reserve ratio multiple were 1.0 rather than 1.5? These kinds of questions can be addressed with UISIM.

Table 4.5 displays summary results from a series of simulations that changed the initial trust fund balances (as of December 31, 1987) in the seven states. As in previous sections, this table shows selected results from the baseline simulation, and then results for a series of departures from the baseline. For each simulation, attention is focused on the need for loans and the final year's (1997) trust fund balance.

The first two departures from the baseline in table 4.5 simply change the initial trust fund balance from its actual December 31, 1987 level to the levels implied by reserve ratio multiples of 1.0 and 1.5. Starting with a reserve multiple of 1.0 raises reserves in six states, all but Florida, and the aggregate increase is $8.3 billion. By 1997, however, observe that reserves in several states are not much above 1997 reserve balances in the baseline. In the aggregate, total 1997 reserves are only $3.6 billion above the baseline, while those in Massachusetts, New Jersey, and California are essentially the same as in the baseline.

When the states are distinguished by the type of experience rating they employ, it becomes clear that reserve ratio and benefit ratio systems respond differently to increases in initial reserves. The benefit ratio

Table 4.5
Simulations with Differing Initial Trust Fund Balances

	Massachusetts	New Jersey	Michigan	Ohio	Florida	Texas	California
Baseline simulation							
Average TUR (%)	5.5	5.5	5.7	5.6	5.5	5.8	5.5
Fund balance – 1997 ($)	1,058	4,272	3,540	3,789	3,648	1,979	8,735
R.R. multiple – 1997	0.31	0.95	0.69	0.82	1.15	0.63	0.75
Initial reserve ratio multiple of 1.0							
Fund balance – 1997 ($)	1,082	4,214	4,770	4,595	3,271	3,936	8,783
R.R. multiple – 1997 ($)	0.31	0.94	0.93	0.99	1.03	1.25	0.76
Initial reserve ratio multiple of 1.5							
Fund balance –1997 ($)	1,068	5,157	6,889	5,324	3,914	4,734	9,676
R.R. multiple – 1997	0.31	1.14	1.35	1.15	1.24	1.50	0.84
Initial RRM of 1.0 and U.S. TURs of the 1980s							
Average TUR (%)	7.3	7.3	7.3	7.3	7.3	7.3	7.3
Loans – 1988-1997 ($)	347	0	0	0	0	0	0
Loans/1992 payroll (%)	0.45	0.00	0.00	0.00	0.00	0.00	0.00
Fund balance – 1997 ($)	806	2,670	4,263	1,971	3,450	4,727	7,478
Initial RRM of 1.0 and state TURs of the 1980s							
Average TUR (%)	5.1	6.3	10.8	8.8	6.4	6.7	7.3
Loans – 1988-1997 ($)	0	0	2,265	2,729	0	0	0
Loans/1992 payroll (%)	0.00	0.00	2.27	2.57	0.00	0.00	0.00
Fund balance – 1997 ($)	1,944	4,621	-159	-1,895	3,555	2,077	7,730
Initial RRM of 1.5 and state TURs of the 1980s							
Average TUR (%)	5.1	6.3	10.8	8.8	6.4	6.7	7.3
Loans – 1988-1997 ($)	0	0	1,057	2,002	0	0	0
Loans/1992 payroll (%)	0.00	0.00	1.06	1.88	0.00	0.00	0.00
Fund balance – 1997 ($)	1,934	5,093	1,123	-1,167	4,198	2,880	7,987

SOURCE: Simulations with UISIM. Loans and reserves measured in millions of dollars. RRM – Reserve Ratio Multiple. TUR – Total Unemployment Rate.

systems in Florida and Texas tend to preserve any initial change in reserves much more completely. In simulations where the states have initial reserve ratio multiples (RRMs) of 1.0, Florida's initial (1987) reserve is $396 million lower and its final (1997) reserve is $377 million lower *vis-a-vis* the baseline. In Texas, the corresponding changes in initial and final balances are increases of $1,737 million and $1,957 million respectively.

That benefit ratio systems should more effectively preserve any initial change in fund balances is not surprising. Because taxes are set primarily on the basis of recent benefit payouts, which are the same in the two simulations, an increase in initial balances does not create any negative feedback on subsequent taxes. In reserve ratio states, a negative feedback from an increase in initial balances reduces employer taxes in later years. This back pressure operates with enough force in Massachusetts, New Jersey and California that nearly all of the initial increase in fund balances is dissipated over the subsequent 10 years, i.e., by 1997.

A similar contrast between reserve ratio and benefit ratio states is observed in simulations that set the initial RRM to 1.5 in each state. Texas and Florida retain essentially all of the increase in initial balances, while the 10-year reserve retention fractions in the four reserve ratio states are as follow: .01 in Massachusetts; .58 in New Jersey; .48 in Ohio; and .24 in California. [17] If these simulations were allowed to run for a 20-year time period, the reserve retention fractions in reserve ratio states would be even lower. Across the seven states, providing each state an initial RRM of 1.5 increases total reserves by $16.8 billion in 1987, but closing reserves in 1997 increase by only $9.8 billion. In the four reserve ratio states, the initial increase in reserves was $10.4 billion, but 1997 reserves increased by only $3.4 billion.

Increases in interest income also produce differential long-run effects in reserve ratio versus benefit ratio states. Higher interest income initially raises the trust fund balance, but then leads to reductions in subsequent employer taxes in reserve ratio states. In benefit ratio states, the increased interest income has no effect on future tax rates, producing larger long-run effects on fund balances.

To test for the relative size of interest effects, a set of simulations were run that differed from the baseline only in the level of the real interest rate. Under a 3 percent real interest rate, as opposed to 1 percent in the baseline, final year (1997) trust fund balances were 14 percent and 16 percent higher than the baseline in Florida and Texas respectively. In the four reserve ratio states, the final trust fund balances were also higher than in the baseline, but the percentage increments were uniformly smaller (ranging from 3 percent to 12 percent). Thus variations in both interest income and in initial trust fund balances have differential i.e., larger, long-run effects on trust fund balances in benefit ratio states than in reserve ratio states.

Turning the focus back to initial trust fund balances, the bottom three panels in table 4.5 show the amount of borrowing associated with differing average unemployment rates. When each state starting with an RRM of 1.0 is subjected to U.S. TURs from the 1980s, only one, Massachusetts, needs any loans ($347 million), and its loans total .45 percent of 1992 payroll. This result can be compared with the result in table 4.3 (the bottom panel), where three states needed loans totaling $1,866 million. Higher initial reserves, an increase of $8.3 billion over the baseline, caused the volume of loans to be $1.5 billion lower when each state was subjected to national TURs from the 1980s.

Recall from table 4.3 that the largest loans were required by Michigan and Ohio when they experienced a repetition of their own TURs from the 1980s. The bottom two panels in table 4.5 show that loans are still needed in these two states even when they have higher initial reserves (but experience a repetition of 1980s state TURs). When the states start with an initial RRM of 1.0 Michigan and Ohio each need more than $2.0 billion. In contrast to table 4.3, however, Texas does not need a loan when its initial RRM is 1.0. Also note that total borrowing, when the initial RRM is 1.0, is only $4,994 million compared to $8,735 million in table 4.3.

Finally, table 4.5 illustrates that a 1.5 reserve ratio multiple (RRM) does not guarantee immunity from the risk of insolvency. In the bottom panel of the table, observe that even with initial RRMs of 1.5, Michigan and Ohio still need loans, loans that exceed 1 percent of 1992 payroll. Admittedly, the average unemployment rates experienced by the two states in the 1980s were unusually high, 10.8 percent and 8.8 percent respectively, but these results indicate that there is nothing foolproof about the 1.5 RRM solvency guideline. On the other hand, observe that total borrowing in this simulation ($3,059 million) is roughly one third of what was needed in simulations that started with actual 1987 trust fund balances.

Based on the results summarized in table 4.5, three conclusions can be drawn. First, a change in initial trust fund balances has much larger long run effects on fund balances in benefit ratio states than in reserve ratio states. This contrast is inherent in the tax rate-setting procedures followed by the two types of experience rating systems. Even if a reserve ratio state achieves a 1.5 RRM, subsequent reserve balances will tend to be reduced through experience rating.[18] Second, higher initial balances reduce both the risk of insolvency and the scale of borrowing in an environment of high unemployment. Individual readers can differ on the advisability of advocating higher balances. To achieve reserve multiples of 1.0 in each of the 7 states, total reserves at the end of 1987 rose by $8.3 billion, roughly double their actual 1987 total. This increase caused total borrowing under a repetition of state TURs from the 1980s to decrease by $3.9 billion. Third, achievement of a 1.5 RRM does not always prevent insolvency and large scale borrowing. The unemployment experiences of Michigan and Ohio in the 1980s were sufficiently adverse that large scale borrowing was indicated even with the large initial balances implied by the 1.5 reserve ratio multiple solvency guideline.

Changes in Benefit Availability

Compared to the 1970s UI benefits are now less available to unemployed workers. In regular UI programs, the ratio of insured unemployment (regular UI claimants or IU) to total unemployment (as measured in the monthly labor force survey or TU) has declined in most states. For each of the seven states being studied in this chapter, there was time series regression evidence of a decline in IU *vis-a-vis* TU after 1981.[19] A reduction in EB availability occurred during the 1981-1983 period following 1981 federal legislation, as new procedures for activating EB became effective. The revised EB triggering mechanism has made extended benefits much less available to the long-term unemployed than in earlier years.

Changes in UI benefit availability have implications for solvency that can be examined with the simulation models. In each state the unemployment scenarios examined in table 4.3 (the baseline and the four time paths of state and national unemployment rates from the 1970s and 1980s) were repeated in environments that approximated the greater UI benefit availability of the 1970s. Specific changes in each state model were to suppress the post-1981 dummy variable shift effect for regular UI and to use the previous (lower) state EB trigger, i.e., a 4 percent insured unemployment rate rather than the present 5 percent rate.[20] The simulations were then rerun over the 1988–1997 period.

Table 4.6 summarizes the simulation results. Because more benefits are now paid out in the baseline simulations, observe in the top panel that the ending (1997) trust fund balances are uniformly lower when compared to the original baseline simulations. The difference is especially large in Michigan ($2,093 million), but it also exceeds $700 million in New Jersey and Ohio. Although ending balances are lower due to the increased benefit availability, no state needs to borrow in these revised baseline simulations.

Under each of the four alternative time paths of the TUR, however, the increases in benefit outlays are large enough to cause a noticeable increase in borrowing. When state TURs of the 1970s are used, four states need loans and borrowing totals $6,530 million (compared to two states needing $1,597 million in corresponding simulations of table 4.3). The same qualitative finding holds in the other three unemployment simulations. Focusing just on total borrowing across the seven states, the other comparisons are as follows: using state TURs from the 1980s, $12,965 million (in table 4.6) versus $8,735 million (in table 4.3);

Table 4.6
Simulations with Benefit Availability of the 1970s

	Massachusetts	New Jersey	Michigan	Ohio	Florida	Texas	California
Baseline simulation							
Average TUR (%)	5.5	5.5	5.7	5.6	5.5	5.8	5.5
Loans – 1988–1997 ($)	0	0	0	0	0	0	0
Fund balance – 1997 ($) original baseline	1,058	4,272	3,540	3,789	3,648	1,979	8,735
1970s benefit availability	901	3,104	1,447	3,064	3,410	1,914	8,328
1970s benefit availability and state TURs of the 1970s							
Average TUR (%)	7.2	7.2	7.9	6.1	6.5	4.8	7.9
Loans – 1988–1997 ($)	1,085	1,000	4,180	0	265	0	0
Loans/1992 payroll (%)	1.42	1.05	4.18	0.00	0.24	0.00	0.00
Fund balance –1997 ($)	-137	-244	-3,773	1,621	3,331	2,044	5,467
1970s benefit availability and state TURs of the 1980s							
Average TUR (%)	5.1	6.3	10.8	8.8	6.4	6.7	7.3
Loans – 1988–1997 ($)	51	0	7,050	5,241	0	623	0
Loans/1992 payroll (%)	0.07	0.00	7.06	4.93	0.00	0.34	0.00
Fund balance – 1997 ($)	1,710	3,176	-5,935	-4,680	3,368	308	7,097
1970s benefit availability and U.S. TURs of the 1970s							
Average TUR (%)	6.2	6.2	6.2	6.2	6.2	6.2	6.2
Loans – 1988–1997 ($)	213	0	531	0	56	332	0
Loans/1992 payroll (%)	0.28	0.00	0.53	0.00	0.05	0.18	0.00
Fund balance – 1997 ($)	391	1,861	-202	1,456	3,605	2,046	6,800
1970s benefit availablity and U.S. TURs of the 1980s							
Average TUR (%)	7.3	7.3	7.3	7.3	7.3	7.3	7.3
Loans – 1988–1997 ($)	879	595	1,872	1,371	0	1,032	0
Loans/1992 payroll (%)	1.15	0.62	1.87	1.29	0.00	0.57	0.00
Fund balance – 1997 ($)	165	1,098	-1,015	-365	3,828	3,121	6,948

SOURCE: Simulations with UISIM. Loans and reserves measured in millions of dollars.

using U.S. TURs from the 1970s, $1,132 million versus $171 million; and using U.S. TURs from the 1980s, $5,749 million versus $1,866 million.

On average the simulations in table 4.6 suggest that with the higher benefit availability of the 1970s the amount of borrowing over the 1988–1997 period would be roughly double what it would be under present benefit availability. Thus the benefit restrictions of the 1980s have important implications for the future solvency of UI programs.[21] Again it should be emphasized that the simulations are not offered as predictions of future borrowing by the states, but rather as the amount of borrowing that would take place if there were no changes in present benefit and tax statutes. The potential future need to borrow and/or to make statutory changes has been reduced by the restrictions in the regular UI and EB programs of the 1980s.

The Effects of Solvency Taxes

In six of the seven states under investigation, all but Massachusetts, the UI tax statutes include provisions for solvency taxes to be activated when the trust fund falls below a certain threshold level.[22] Of the possible elements of an automatic pay-as-you-go funding strategy, solvency taxes are the most prevalent. In 1988, 28 UI programs could automatically activate a solvency tax, whereas only 3 provided for automatic tax base changes, and only 8 provided for automatic benefit restrictions when trust funds fell below predetermined thresholds.

Solvency tax provisions vary widely from one state to the next. The terminology used to describe these taxes in individual states also can be a source of confusion. What is termed a solvency tax in Massachusetts, described in chapter 3, is in fact a tax to cover noncharges and ineffective charges. This is not a solvency tax as the term is being used in this chapter. In Michigan the tax statute identifies as a solvency tax a levy on negative balance employers which is used to pay the interest on new UI loans (a tax whose rate varies from 0 to 2 percent of taxable payroll depending on the size of the outstanding loan balance). Michigan's Accounting Building Component (ABC) of the UI tax is a solvency tax, which is activated whenever trust fund reserves (as of the tax computation date) are smaller than 3.75 percent of total payroll. The receipts for the ABC tax go into the state's trust fund, whereas solvency tax receipts go into an interest account which is separate from the trust fund. For the present discussion, we will consider as solvency taxes only those taxes designed to increase the trust fund balance, hence to avoid borrowing or lessen the size of loans. Other taxes such as interest taxes are no less real to the affected employers, but they do not affect UI trust fund balances.

Four features can be identified that affect the performance of solvency taxes: (1) the threshold trust fund level that activates the tax; (2) the range of statutory tax rates; (3) the proportion of employers affected; and (4) the possibility of negative as well as positive solvency tax adjustments. Across the six states, the trust fund thresholds range from a high of 3.75 percent of total payroll in Michigan to a low of a zero fund balance in New Jersey. The range of maximum statutory tax rate increases varies from lows of .7 percent in New Jersey and .8 percent in California to highs of 3.0 percent in Michigan and 3.4 percent in Ohio. When the solvency tax is activated, it may raise all statutory tax rates (thus affecting all employers) or it may increase the range of rates by raising the maximum statutory rate. In the latter situation, only some employers will actually experience higher rates (those at the previous maximum tax rate). In four states (New Jersey, Ohio, Florida, and California), all statutory rates are increased by the solvency tax while in two (Michigan and Texas), the tax increases the maximum statutory rate. Four states activate their solvency tax only to increase revenues when the fund balance is low (New Jersey, Michigan, Ohio, and California), while two (Florida and Texas), use the tax to both reduce and increase revenues.[23] In the latter two states, solvency taxes act to raise the fund balance when it is low and to reduce the balance when it is high.

Recall that the UI tax provisions in Michigan use both benefit ratios and reserve ratios to determine individual employer tax rates. The lagged five-year average of the benefit ratio is the principal explanatory variable in the employer tax rate equation. The lagged benefit ratio operates so strongly that the maximum statutory tax rate (the rate influenced by the ABC tax) did not enter the tax rate regression with a significantly positive effect.[24] Over the past 20 years, Michigan's trust fund balance has always fallen below the current solvency tax trigger threshold (3.75 percent of total payroll for its ABC tax), so that all relevant recent experience is with the solvency tax turned "on." This was also found to hold for all years in the baseline simulation.

Because Michigan did not provide recent experiences of a period with the solvency tax (the ABC tax) being turned "off," we constructed estimates of the importance of these taxes within the overall tax rate structure. The procedure involved three steps. After examining data provided by the state on the distribution of taxable wages by benefit ratios, we concluded that about 15 percent of taxable wages were from employers whose benefit ratios exceeded 6 percent. Their taxable wages were then multiplied by a representative ABC tax rate, i.e., 1.5 percent, the midpoint between 0 and 3 percent. The resulting estimate of ABC tax revenues was then subtracted from total tax revenues. These estimates typically accounted for 5 to 10 percent of total tax revenues in Michigan.

In Texas, where the solvency tax (the deficit tax) also affects the maximum statutory tax rate, the maximum tax rate has only a small impact on the effective employer tax rate.[25] Thus, of the six states under investigation that have solvency taxes, the models do not have econometric estimates of their effect on revenues in one (Michigan), and it is probable that their estimated effects on revenues may be understated in one (Texas). More confidence can be placed in the estimated effects of solvency taxes in the four states where changes in solvency taxes affect all employers, not just employers subject to the maximum statutory tax rate, i.e., New Jersey, Ohio, Florida, and California.

To examine the quantitative importance of solvency taxes, simulations were conducted where solvency taxes were removed from each state's 1988 tax rate structures. There were five simulations in each state, which repeated the time paths of the unemployment rate as in table 4.3 (the baseline rate of 5.5 percent and the four combinations of state and national unemployment rates from the 1970s and the 1980s). Table 4.7 summarizes the simulation results.

None of the six states needs loans in the new baseline simulations. In New Jersey and California, states with large initial balances, removal

Table 4.7
Unemployment Simulations with Solvency Taxes Suppressed

	New Jersey	Michigan	Ohio	Florida	Texas	California
Baseline simulation						
Loans – 1988–1997 ($)	0	0	0	0	0	0
Fund balance – 1997 ($)	4,272	2,814	3,085	3,986	1,835	8,735
Change from table 4.3	0	−726	−704	338	−144	0
State unemployment rates of the 1970s						
Loans – 1988–1997 ($)	0	1,477	0	0	0	0
Change from table 4.3	0	669	0	0	0	0
Fund balance –1997 ($)	1,408	−1,109	1,338	3,619	2,052	5,439
Change from table 4.3	0	−750	−1,201	72	−56	−996
State unemployment rates of the 1980s						
Loans – 1988–1997 ($)	4,438	4,604	5,296	0	849	0
Change from table 4.3	0	288	1,343	0	383	0
Fund balance – 1997 ($)	0	−2,835	−4,940	4,096	−26	7,816
Change from table 4.3	0	−625	−1,821	163	−457	97
U.S. unemployment rates of the 1970s						
Loans – 1988–1997 ($)	0	0	0	0	335	0
Change from table 4.3	0	0	0	0	164	0
Fund balance – 1997 ($)	3,063	1,498	1,097	3,779	1,781	7,524
Change from table 4.3	0	−968	−1,293	170	−340	0
U.S. unemployment rates of the 1980s						
Loans – 1988–1997 ($)	0	0	1,570	0	1,103	0
Change from table 4.3	0	0	1,134	0	152	0
Fund balance – 1997 ($)	2,469	726	−854	3,808	2,628	7,454
Change from table 4.3	0	−1,057	−1,898	−20	−398	−2

SOURCE: Simulations with UISIM. Loans and reserves measured in millions of dollars.

of the solvency taxes has no effect because the trust fund balances remain consistently above the thresholds that activate their solvency taxes. The largest effects on the 1997 trust fund balances in the baseline are found in Michigan and Ohio, states with low initial balances and a wide range (3.0 and 3.4 percentage points respectively) of solvency tax rates.[26] Note also that removal of the solvency tax in Florida causes its 1997 trust fund balance to increase because tax rates are no longer held down by the solvency tax.[27] In all four states where 1997 fund balances are affected, the size of the effect is modest.

When the states are subjected to a repetition of state and national unemployment rates from the 1970s and 1980s, the absence of solvency taxes increases the volume of borrowing and reduces the 1997 trust fund balance (except for Florida). Note, however, that the effects are generally small. In New Jersey, which has the lowest solvency tax trigger threshold (a zero fund balance), there is no effect in any simulation. The largest effects are found in Ohio when the state experiences a repetition of state TURs from the 1980s and national TURs from the 1980s. Removal of Ohio's solvency tax increases total borrowing by more than $1 billion in both simulations and causes the 1997 trust fund balance to be $1.8–$1.9 billion lower. The effects on loans and 1997 fund balances are smaller in the other states, with Michigan consistently ranked second in the size of the solvency (ABC) tax effects.

Perhaps the most interesting finding to be noted in the table 4.7 simulations is that solvency taxes in these six states do not prevent insolvency. For departures of unemployment from baseline unemployment there are 24 simulations in table 4.7. In seven of the twenty-four, the state needs UI loans. In all seven instances, the state also needed loans when the identical simulation was run with the solvency tax present, i.e., in table 4.3. For these states, solvency taxes operate to modestly reduce the scale of borrowing, but they did not prevent insolvency.[28] The simulation results suggest that solvency taxes are not of much quantitative importance.

The table 4.7 simulations point to two main conclusions. First, the solvency taxes presently operative in the six states have only modest effects on UI trust fund balances and the need for UI loans. Second, the effects of solvency taxes were largest in Ohio. If solvency taxes are to have larger effects than the effects found here, they need to be structured with a more aggressive combination of higher trigger thresholds, a wider range of statutory rates, and applicability to all employers.

Tax Responsiveness

To maintain solvency and avoid large-scale borrowing, individual states will place differing degrees of emphasis on pre-funding, automatic pay-as-you-go, and discretionary pay-as-you-go financing strategies. A key requirement of a successful automatic pay-as-you-go strategy is that tax receipts (and perhaps benefit outlays) respond rapidly and strongly when recession-induced claims for UI benefits increase. A rapid and strong tax response is even more important if a state enters a recession with a small trust fund balance.

In the final simulation analysis of the present chapter, each of the seven states was subjected to a modest but sustained increase in UI claims, and the resulting response of UI taxes was noted. The analysis was quite limited in scope, e.g., benefit responsiveness and tax base responsiveness were not analyzed, and large scale changes in claims were not analyzed. By examining all seven states, however, contrasts between reserve ratio and benefit ratio experience rating systems could be observed.

The analysis of tax responsiveness was conducted using the unemployment rates from the baseline simulations as the point of departure. In each state, the level of average unemployment rate was increased by .5 percentage points from 1988 through 1997 (from 5.5 percent to 6.0 percent for most observations). [29] To remove the effects of differing initial trust fund reserves, the simulations were conducted with similar initial balances across states. Initial reserves were set to equal a reserve ratio multiple of 1.0 and also a multiple of .2. The latter reserve position is of more interest, since a rapid and strong tax response is especially important when reserves are low if insolvency is to be avoided. By contrasting the tax responses under differing initial reserve positions, some insight into the quantitative importance of solvency taxes may be gained.

Table 4.8 summarizes the simulation results showing changes in benefits, changes in taxes, and tax responsiveness ratios (the ratio of tax changes to benefit changes) in each state. Tax responses to a sustained increase in unemployment are shown after five years and after ten years. Responses are displayed for both the high and the low initial reserve positions.

At least four important findings are apparent in table 4.8. (1) The short-run responses of taxes are smaller than the long-run responses.[30] (2) Short-run tax responses are larger in the two benefit ratio states (Florida and Texas) than in the reserve ratio states. (3) Short-run and long-run tax responses exhibit less variation in benefit ratio states. The uneven response of taxes in reserve ratio states is to be expected, as trust fund thresholds are crossed and then a different (higher) statutory tax rate schedule is activated. (4) Perhaps most significant is the finding that tax responsiveness ratios, both 5-year and 10-year ratios, are not consistently larger in simulations with low initial trust fund balances. The responses are larger in some states where solvency taxes are operative, e.g., Ohio and Texas, but even in those states the differences (for low vis-a-vis high initial reserves) are of limited size.

Two main conclusions can be drawn from the table 4.8 simulations. First, taxes in benefit ratio states (with three-year averaging periods) respond more quickly and consistently to changes in benefit outlays than do taxes in reserve ratio states. Second, solvency taxes do not add much to the responsiveness of taxes when benefit payments increase but initial trust fund balances are low. Automatic pay-as-you-go tax features do not operate with much strength in these seven states.

Table 4.8
Simulations of Tax Responsiveness

	Massachusetts	New Jersey	Michigan	Ohio	Florida	Texas	California
5-year response, initial RRM of 1.0							
Change in benefits	282	357	353	464	299	557	687
Change in taxes	155	240	50	49	226	406	34
Ratio of tax change to benefit change	0.550	0.672	0.142	0.106	0.756	0.729	0.049
10-year response, initial RRM of 1.0							
Change in benefits	635	798	823	1,105	723	1,355	1,553
Change in taxes	557	616	900	389	669	1,332	1,260
Ratio of tax change to benefit change	0.877	0.772	1.094	0.352	0.925	0.983	0.811
5-year response, initial RRM of 0.2							
Change in benefits	282	357	353	464	299	557	687
Change in taxes	187	95	41	139	226	440	335
Ratio of tax change to benefit change	0.663	0.266	0.116	0.300	0.756	0.790	0.488
10-year response, initial RRM of 0.2							
Change in benefits	635	798	823	1,105	723	1,355	1,553
Change in taxes	540	227	276	598	669	1,357	942
Ratio of tax change to benefit change	0.850	0.284	0.335	0.541	0.925	1.001	0.607

SOURCE: Simulations with UISIM. Benefits and taxes measured in millions of dollars. RRM – Reserve Ratio Multiple. In each simulation the unemployment rate was increased by .5 percentage points per year above the unemployment rate in the baseline simulation.

Conclusions

The preceding simulation analyses have yielded several findings regarding UI trust fund adequacy. Probably the most important conclusion of the chapter, however, is that the simulation models developed for the seven states have proven useful for examining a number of issues related to fund adequacy. UISIM is a useful and flexible analytic tool.

The detailed findings of the chapter can be grouped into three categories: obvious, less obvious, and new findings. Obvious findings include the following. Large initial trust fund balances help to prevent insolvency and the need for large-scale borrowing. Modest increases in state unemployment above full employment levels, i.e., unemployment rates of 5.5. percent, do not cause important financing problems for the states. Major borrowing and large-scale indebtedness were observed in the states that had the largest increases in average unemployment. Finally, symmetric treatment in the responses of taxes and benefits to inflation helps to reduce the risk of insolvency.

Among the less obvious findings, the following two should be noted. First, the threat to solvency of asymmetric treatment of maximum weekly benefits and the tax base in the face of higher inflation is not direct but indirect. High inflation by itself reduces reserve adequacy in states that index just the maximum weekly benefit. This reduction in reserve adequacy, i.e., the reserve ratio, makes the effect of higher unemployment more serious than it otherwise would be. Second, the two major experience rating systems operate differently over 10-year periods. Reserve ratio systems do not preserve changes in fund balances as completely in the long run as do benefit ratio systems.

Four new findings are the following. (1) The 1.5 reserve ratio multiple is not an infallible solvency guideline. Michigan and Ohio both required large-scale loans under a repetition of unemployment experiences from the 1980s, even in simulations where they started with 1.5 multiples. (2) Restrictions on benefit availability in the 1980s have major implications for the future solvency of UI programs. The restrictions roughly halved the volume of borrowing when compared to simulations with the higher benefit availability of the 1970s. (3) Solvency taxes had only modest effects on the volume of borrowing. These taxes did not prevent insolvency, and they exerted only a small effect on the response of taxes to increases in benefit outlays. (4) The short-run response of taxes to increases in benefit outlays was larger in benefit ratio states than in reserve ratio states, and the response was also less varied in benefit ratio states.

Large reserves and responsive tax systems both help to prevent insolvency in UI programs. In the simulations of this chapter, enough instances of insolvency and large-scale borrowing were found to assure the continued importance of solvency questions in future years.

NOTES

1. Nationwide, 32 of 53 programs secured UI loans sometime between 1980 and 1987, and 15 programs needed large loans, i.e., loans exceeding 1 percent of 1984 covered payroll.

2. Across the 52 jurisdictions that experience rated employer taxes in 1988, 32 used reserve ratios, 13 used benefit ratios, 2 (Michigan and Pennsylvania) used both reserve ratios and benefit ratios, and 5 used other experience rating systems.

3. In 1988, 17 programs indexed both the weekly benefit maximum and the taxable wage base, 16 states indexed neither and 19 states indexed the weekly benefit maximum but not the tax base. Only Alaska indexed the taxable wage base but not the weekly benefit maximum.

4. In California, the year end trust fund balance determines which tax schedule is operative on January 1 of the next year. Florida uses the current calendar year as one of the three years in the benefit ratio computation to set the next year's tax rates. These two states also have other tax setting provisions which entail longer time lags.

5. Economists differ in their opinion of what constitutes full employment, with many thinking it lies in the range from 5.5 percent to 6.0 percent. The simulation analysis assumes the full employment unemployment rate to be 5.5 percent.

6. Some readers may think only the results showing departures from baseline levels are meaningful, but not the baseline levels themselves.

7. This was done to prevent a sharp drop in claims in the first year of the simulations, i.e., an excessively large effect of lagged unemployment in the insured unemployment equations.

8. Average weekly wages increased at a compound annual growth rate of 6.2 percent between 1967 and 1987.

9. Texas completed its UI debt repayments in 1988, while Michigan continued to make repayments after 1988. The baseline simulations assumed that Texas completed its repayments of old debt in early 1989 and that Michigan completed its debt repayments in 1991.

10. The Texas formula raises the maximum by $7 for each $10 increase in average weekly wages in manufacturing.

11. Only two of the fourteen state decade averages fell below 5.5 percent: Texas in the 1970s (4.8 percent) and Massachusetts in the 1980s (5.1 percent).

12. We examined data for each of the three states in the following way. The difference between annual receipts (taxes plus interest) and benefits (regular benefits plus the state share of EB) was compared to gross interest bearing loans and net loans (gross loans less repayments). In years when receipts were less than benefits (and the net trust fund balance was negative), net loans were about half of gross loans.

13. The three states' 1988 unemployment rates, which are used for 1997 in these simulations, were as follows: Massachusetts 3.3 percentl; New Jersey 3.8 percent; and Florida 5.0 percent.

14. Average weekly wages grew by 9.5 percent and 9.0 percent in 1980 and 1981, by 4.0 percent to 4.4 percent between 1983 and 1986, and by 4.4 and 5.0 percent respectively in 1987 and 1988.

15. The national averages of annual wage inflation in the 1970s (1970–1979) and 1980s (1979–1988) as measured by average weekly wages in covered employment were respectively 6.5 percent and 6.0 percent.

16. The simulations do suggest that California experiences some loss of reserve adequacy under increased wage inflation. The 1997 reserve ratio in the simulation with 10.0 percent inflation is 61.0 percent of its baseline level (1.08 percent versus 1.77 percent), whereas the maximum benefit.weekly wage ratio is 69.1 percent of its baseline level (.220 versus .318). Experiments with additional average inflation rates, e.g., 9 percent and 12 percent, showed that the two ratios did not decline at the same rate as the inflation rate increased. Because the reserve ratio did decline more rapidly, there was evidence of a modest loss of reserve adequacy, but smaller than in the states with asymmetric treatment of indexation.

17. These retention fractions for simulations with initial reserve ratio multiples (RRMs) of 1.5 were calculated by comparing changes in ending balances as of 1997 with changes in initial balances as of 1987. For example, in Massachusetts the actual 1987 balance of $1097 million became $2700 million under an RRM of 1.5, or an initial increment of $1,603 million. The final year increment of only $10 million ($1,068 million less $1,058 million) was only .01 of the starting year increment.

18. This statement holds under the present (1988) tax schedules operative in the four reserve ratio experience rating states (Massachusetts, New Jersey, Ohio, and California). If new (higher) schedules were imposed, they could be structured so that RRMs of 1.5 could be sustained in the long run.

19. As noted previously, the evidence came from time series regressions where IU was regressed on TU, TU lagged one year, and a dummy variable that equaled 1 for 1981 and later years. The dummy variable coefficient was negative in each of the 7 states. The downward shifts in IU implied by the dummy variable coefficients ranged from 8 percent in California to 51 percent in Florida.

20. The insured unemployment rate (IUR) is the ratio of insured unemployment to UI covered employment and expressed as a percentage. Because the IUR measures used in the models did not include EB recipients in the pre 1980s years, the simulations understate somewhat the actual reduction in EB availability caused by the 1981 changes in the EB triggers.

21. Reductions in benefit availability also have implications for the performance of UI as a macroeconomic automatic stabilizer and as a microeconomic income maintenance program. Restricting benefit availability, which enhances future solvency prospects, at the same time impairs the program's income maintenance performance at both the macro level and the micro level.

22. The solvency taxes are as follows: (1) New Jersey's 10 percent addition to the tax rates of tax schedule E when the trust fund balance turns negative; (2) Michigan's ABC (account building component) tax; (3) Ohio's MSL (minimum safe level) tax; (4) the deficit tax and the tax credit applicable in Texas; (5) the fund balance adjustment factor, part of the variable adjustment factor, in Florida; and (6) California's 15 percent addition to the tax rates of tax schedule F when the fund balance falls below .8 percent of total payroll.

23. Texas activates its deficit tax when the fund balance falls below 1 percent of taxable payroll. A tax reduction (credit) is activated when the fund balance exceeds 2 percent of taxable payroll. Florida applies its fund balance adjustment factor symmetrically to upward and downward departures of the trust fund balance from 5 percent of taxable payroll.

24. The only other tax variable found to enter the tax rate equation with a significant effect (when the benefit ratio was present) was the minimum statutory tax rate (the noncharged benefits tax or NBC tax). Appendix C shows the tax rate regression equation. The benefit ratio and the reserve ratio were too highly correlated to both enter the tax rate equation at the same time, and of the two, the benefit ratio was always the more powerful explanatory variable.

25. The coefficient for the maximum statutory tax rate was .043 in the Texas effective tax rate equation, whereas the lagged benefit ratio had a coefficient of 1.474. The equation appears in appendix B.

26. The effects are largest in Michigan and Ohio when measured relative to total payroll, as well as the absolute effects shown in table 4.7.

27. Recall that solvency taxes can operate to reduce as well as increase tax revenues in Florida and Texas.

28. When Michigan experienced a repetition of U.S. TURs from the 1980s, there was a 4-year period when the net trust fund balance fell below $100 million. In the corresponding simulation that included the solvency (ABC) tax, the fund balance averaged about $250 million higher during these four years.

29. In Michigan, Ohio, and Texas, where unemployment rates exceeded 5.5 percent in the first one or two years of the simulations, the unemployment rates where also raised by .5 percentage points in these initial years.

30. Recall that in reserve ratio states there is the strong tendency for high initial reserves to be dissipated in the long run. (Recall table 4.5.) The findings in table 4.8 do not contradict this, because tax changes are measured as departures from a baseline where reserve-induced tax reductions take place.

5
Regional Unemployment
and Insolvency

Chapter 1 examined national data on UI loans, debt, and repayment activities in the 1970s and 1980s. Disaggregation of the national data by geographic area reveals a number of clearcut patterns. In both decades, borrowing and indebtedness have been closely linked to regional unemployment developments. This chapter examines regional aspects of UI financing problems. It starts with a review of regional borrowing patterns.

UI Loans by Census Division

Table 5.1 displays summary data on UI loans for three time periods: 1972 to 1979, 1980 to 1983, and 1984 to 1987. The UI programs have been grouped into the nine census divisions, with Puerto Rico and the Virgin Islands assigned to the Mid-Atlantic division.[1] The table shows the dollar amounts and percentage distribution of loans, number of programs needing loans, and loans as a percent of payrolls for the nine divisions and the entire United States.

Although 26 of the 27 census divisions—time period cells in the table show positive loan amounts (all but the Pacific division in 1980–1983), the dollar amounts in each of the three periods are heavily concentrated in a few divisions. States in the North East accounted for 59.8 percent of borrowing in the 1970s and ten of eleven jurisdictions (all but New Hampshire) required loans sometime between 1972 and 1979. Between 1980 and 1983, loan activity was concentrated in the Midwest, 65.2 percent of all loans and borrowing by nine of twelve programs. The Midwest also accounted for the largest share of loans in the 1984–1987 period (44.4 percent), but states in the South also accounted

Table 5.1
UI Loans by Census Division, 1972 to 1987

| | North East | | Midwest | | South | | | West | | United |
Loan activities	New England	Mid-Atlantic	East North Central	West North Central	South Atlantic	East South Central	West South Central	Mountain	Pacific	States
					Loans from 1972 to 1979					
Total loans	974	2,393	1,572	172	225	57	30	18	190	5,632
Percent of total	17.3	42.5	27.9	3.1	4.0	1.0	0.5	0.3	3.4	100.0
Programs	5	5	3	1	4	1	1	2	3	25
Loans as a percent of 1975 payroll	2.89	2.07	1.26	0.43	0.28	0.20	0.06	0.08	0.23	0.97
					Loans from 1980 to 1983					
Total loans	95	2,668	8,763	960	407	368	1,451	189	0	14,901
Percent of total	0.6	17.9	58.8	6.4	2.7	2.5	9.7	1.3	0.0	100.0
Programs	4	3	5	4	5	3	3	3	0	30
Loans as a percent of 1981 payroll	0.14	1.35	4.06	1.27	0.25	0.68	1.12	0.35	0.00	1.32
					Loans from 1984 to 1987					
Total loans	5	1,682	3,323	711	231	81	2,898	89	62	9,080
Percent of total	0.1	18.5	36.6	7.8	2.5	0.9	31.9	1.0	0.7	100.0
Programs	1	2	4	3	2	1	2	3	1	19
Loans as a percent of 1985 payroll	0.01	0.65	1.23	0.73	0.10	0.12	1.86	0.12	0.03	0.61

SOURCE: U.S. Depaprtment of Labor, UI Service, "Title XII Advances and Repayments," various issues. Loans measured in thousands of dollars. Puerto Rico and the Virgin Islands included in the Mid-Atlantic.

for over one-third (35.3 percent) of the total. The increased borrowing in the South during 1984–1987 took place primarily in Louisiana and Texas, as petroleum extraction and production declined.

When loans are measured as a percent of payrolls, the borrowing in each division can be compared to the national average. In all three periods, loans as a percent of payrolls were consistently low (less than three-tenths of the national average) in the South Atlantic, Mountain and Pacific divisions, but above average in the East North Central division. In each of the three periods, one division had loans (as a percent of payrolls) that were about three times the national average: the New England division in 1972–1979, the East North Central division in 1980–1983, and the West South Central division in 1984–1987.

The changes in the positions of the New England and West South Central divisions between 1972–1979 and 1984–1987 are especially dramatic. Across the nine divisions, loans as a percent of payrolls during 1972–1979 were highest in New England (2.89 percent) and lowest in the West South Central (1.06 percent). In 1984–1987, however, their rankings were exactly reversed; they were highest in the West South Central (1.86 percent) and lowest in New England (.01 percent). Considering all three periods covered by table 5.1, it is clear that the geographic concentration of UI loan activities was not stable in the 1970s and 1980s.

Regional Economic Performance

The geographic patterns of UI loan activity in the 1970s and 1980s have been strongly influenced by changes in the fortunes of the various regional economies. This section reviews regional labor market performance since World War II with attention directed to the four major regions as defined by the Census Bureau: the North East, Midwest, South and West.[2]

When one examines regional labor market data in the period since World War II, four "facts" become apparent. (1) Business cycle indicators in the regional economies reflect the overall U.S. business cycle. (2) Economic performance in the regions can depart substantially from national economic performance, and the departures can last for several consecutive years. (3) The relative economic fortunes of individual regions can undergo large changes in short periods of time. (4) Employment growth in the South and West has been consistently higher than employment growth in the North East and Midwest.

The long-run employment growth disparities by region can be illustrated as follows. Between 1948 and 1987, the share of private, nonfarm employment located in the North East fell from 33.1 percent to 22.9 percent while in the Midwest it declined from 31.6 percent to 24.7 percent. The rates of decline of these regions' shares, however, were not uniform, as shown by data from the 1980s. Between 1979 and 1987, the employment share for the North East was stable at roughly 23.0 percent, while the share for the Midwest declined from 27.3 percent to 24.7 percent, more than twice as fast as during the previous 30 years.

To characterize regional labor market performance, two types of indicators will be examined: unemployment and employment growth. Two measures of unemployment are the total unemployment rate (TUR) from the monthly labor force survey (the CPS) and the insured unemployment rate (IUR) from UI program data. The employment variable is private, nonfarm employment from the U.S. Labor Department's establishment survey. Note that attention is focused on real variables and not on labor market prices, i.e., wage rates. Each of the three labor market indicators is measured at both the regional and national level, allowing one to judge the similarity of their movements as well as the size and persistence of regional deviations from national developments.

To illustrate the association between regional unemployment and national unemployment, table 5.2 presents annual data on TURs for the 1967–1987 period. The table displays both absolute and relative unemployment rates for the four regions. The national business cycle is apparent in the four regional unemployment rates, each of which has peaks in 1975 and again in 1982-83. Over the 1967–1987 period, the averages for three of the four regions are close to the national average, while the West displays a somewhat higher average (7.2 percent versus 6.4 percent for the U.S.).

Table 5.2
National and Regional Unemployment Rates, 1967 to 1987

Year	Total unemployment rates for all persons 16 and older					Relative unemployment rates (regional rate/U.S. rate)			
	United States	North East	Midwest	South	West	North East	Midwest	South	West
1967	3.8	3.5	3.3	3.9	5.5	0.92	0.87	1.03	1.45
1968	3.6	3.2	3.0	3.7	4.9	0.89	0.83	1.03	1.36
1969	3.5	3.2	2.9	3.6	4.9	0.91	0.83	1.03	1.40
1970	4.9	4.6	4.5	4.6	6.9	0.94	0.92	0.94	1.41
1971	5.9	6.2	5.5	4.9	8.1	1.05	0.93	0.83	1.37
1972	5.6	6.3	5.0	4.8	7.1	1.13	0.89	0.86	1.27
1973	4.9	5.5	4.4	4.1	6.5	1.12	0.90	0.84	1.33
1974	5.6	6.1	4.8	5.1	6.8	1.09	0.86	0.91	1.21
1975	8.5	9.5	7.9	7.7	9.2	1.12	0.93	0.91	1.08
1976	7.7	9.4	6.6	6.8	8.7	1.22	0.86	0.88	1.13
1977	7.1	8.4	6.0	6.4	7.8	1.18	0.85	0.90	1.10
1978	6.1	6.9	5.3	5.6	6.6	1.13	0.87	0.92	1.08
1979	5.8	6.6	5.5	5.4	6.0	1.14	0.95	0.93	1.03
1980	7.1	7.1	8.2	6.4	6.9	1.00	1.15	0.90	0.97
1981	7.6	7.4	8.6	7.0	7.4	0.97	1.13	0.92	0.97
1982	9.7	9.0	11.1	8.9	9.9	0.93	1.14	0.92	1.02
1983	9.6	8.7	10.8	9.3	9.5	0.91	1.13	0.97	0.99
1984	7.5	6.8	8.4	7.2	7.6	0.91	1.12	0.96	1.01
1985	7.2	6.2	8.0	7.2	7.3	0.86	1.11	1.00	1.01
1986	7.0	5.6	7.3	7.6	7.1	0.80	1.04	1.09	1.01
1987	6.2	4.5	6.7	6.8	6.3	0.73	1.08	1.10	1.02
1967–87 average	6.4	6.4	6.4	6.0	7.2	1.00	0.97	0.95	1.15
1967–87 range	6.2	6.3	8.2	5.7	5.0	0.50	0.33	0.28	0.48

SOURCE: All unemployment rates are from the CPS. Regional detail is published in the *Geographic Profile of Employment and Unemployment.*

When the regional relative unemployment rates are examined, however, a number of systematic patterns become apparent that provide clear evidence of the varied experiences of the regional economies. Over the 21 years, each region has experienced the highest of the four regional unemployment rates in at least two years, and three regions (all but the West) have experienced the lowest of the four regional unemployment rates in at least five years. The West has had the highest average relative unemployment rate over these 21 years, and the South has had the lowest average.

More important than the averages of the relative unemployment rates are their variability over time and their strong patterns of serial correlation. For each region, the range of variation in its relative unemployment rate exceeded .25 between 1967 and 1987, and for two (the North East and the West) the range exceed .45. The strong serial correlation in the relative unemployment rates is striking. The highest relative unemployment rates were found the in the West from 1967 to 1974, the North East from 1975 to 1979, the Midwest from 1980 to 1985, and the South from 1986 to 1987. Strong serial correlation in the lowest relative unemployment rates is also obvious in table 5.2. Since the late 1960s, the unemployment rates in the regions have not moved in lock step with the national unemployment rate, and regional deviations have typically persisted for multiyear periods.

Table 5.2 also provides evidence of rapid short-run changes in regional relative unemployment rates. Examples of rapid increases in relative unemployment are provided by the North East between 1970 and 1972, the Midwest between 1978 and 1980, and the South between 1984 and 1986. Rapid declines in relative unemployment occurred in the North East between 1979 and 1980 and in the West between 1973 and 1975.

To characterize regional labor market performance in a more systematic manner, each of the three regional labor market indicators (the TUR, the IUR, and the private, nonfarm employment share) was regressed on its respective national counterpart. The goodness of fit, i.e., R^2, of the regressions provides evidence of the coincidence of regional with national economic developments. The errors from the regressions show the size and direction of regional deviations from the national economy. Because regional TURs are only available since 1967, the TUR regressions cover just the 1967–1987 period. Both sets of unemployment regressions were fitted as homogeneous equations, i.e., without constant terms. The slope coefficients from the equations show the proportional relationship between regional unemployment and the national unemployment rate. The employment shares equations were fitted with a linear time trend to test for the smoothness of change in regional employment shares over the 1948–1987 period.

Table 5.3 shows the regressions and summary statistics. All 12 of the R^2s exceed .50 and nine exceed .80. Unemployment in each of the four regions is positively associated with national unemployment. The constants of proportionality range from .824 (the IUR regression in the South) to 1.191 (the IUR regression in the North East). Both sets of unemployment regressions suggest that unemployment in the West is less closely associated with national unemployment than is unemployment in the other three regions. When regional unemployment coefficients are compared across the four TUR equations, they mirror the patterns previously noted in table 5.2, i.e., TURs were highest in the West and lowest in the South over the 1967–1987 period.

When the IUR and TUR regressions for each region are compared, they reveal systematic differences in UI benefit availability by region. Coefficients in the IUR regressions are larger than for the TUR regressions in both the North East and West, but smaller in both the Midwest and the South. In the North East and the West, UI benefits are relatively more accessible than they are in the Midwest and the South.[3]

Strong trends in the employment shares of all four regions are apparent in the employment share regressions. The employment share trended downward most rapidly in the North East and upward most rapidly in the South between 1948 and 1987. Note that all four employment share regressions have R^2s that exceed .90. Large scale trendwise changes in employment shares occurred in all four regions during these 40 years.

The regional unemployment rate and employment share regressions provide a basis for judging the degree of regional variation around national economic performance. In the unemployment equations, unusually

Table 5.3
Regressions to Explain Regional Unemployment and Employment Indicators

Region	Independent variables				Summary measures			
	Constant	National IUR	National TUR	Time trend	R^2	Standard error	D.W.	Mean of dep. var.
Dependent variable: regional IUR – insured unemployment rate, 1948-1987								
North East		1.191 (74.3)			0.924	0.384	0.56	4.323
Midwest		0.897 (39.9)			0.812	0.540	0.54	3.220
South		0.824 (53.5)			0.892	0.370	0.37	2.949
West		1.155 (39.1)			0.646	0.709	0.48	4.280
Dependent variable: regional TUR – total unemployment rate, 1967-1987								
North East			0.997 (33.8)		0.782	0.899	0.19	6.414
Midwest			1.010 (37.7)		0.876	0.817	0.25	6.371
South			0.940 (64.0)		0.927	0.447	0.38	6.047
West			1.092 (37.0)		0.564	0.900	0.16	7.191
Dependent variable: establishment survey private nonfarm employment percentage, 1948-1987								
North East	33.47 (192.0)			-0.294 (39.6)	0.976	0.541	0.15	27.45
Midwest	32.54 (181.8)			-0.184 (24.2)	0.937	0.555	0.22	28.78
South	22.54 (161.8)			0.261 (44.1)	0.980	0.432	0.19	27.90
West	11.44 (100.1)			0.216 (44.5)	0.981	0.355	0.18	15.88

SOURCE: All data published by the U.S. Department of Labor. Beneath each coefficient appears the absolute value of its t ratio.

strong regional performance is suggested in years when the regression overpredicts the regional unemployment rate. Strong regional employment performance is suggested in years when a region's employment share is underpredicted.

Table 5.4 uses fitted values from the regression equations of table 5.3 to judge regional labor market performance. In each region, weak performance is inferred when an index ratio exceeds 1.00 and vice versa. The indices for the fitted unemployment series (the TUR and the IUR) are ratios of actual to predicted unemployment rates. For employment, the indices are ratios of predicted shares to actual employment shares. Each region has three ratios from 1967 to 1987, but only two from 1948 to 1966. Note that the performance indices based on the IUR and TUR regressions show more variability than the indices based on the employment regressions. To highlight years of unusually good and unusually weak performance low and high ratios that depart substantially from 1.00 are identified with +'s and *'s respectively. The identifiers are applied to IUR and TUR indices which deviate by at least .10 from 1.00 and employment share indices which deviate by at least .03 from 1.00.

Over the 40 years covered by table 5.4, each region has experienced major changes in relative labor market performance. The indices for the North East show weak performance from 1972 to 1979, but then strong performance from 1982 to 1987. In this region and the others, there is strong serial correlation in the performance indices, i.e., good years are bunched together as are bad years. There is also a clear tendency for the employment-based index to lag somewhat behind the unemployment indices. Strong economic performance in the Midwest is indicated in many years between 1948 and 1980, particularly in non-recession years. Durable manufacturing employment, which is extremely volatile over the business cycle, has traditionally been concentrated in this region. Note how the midwestern performance indices change in the recession years 1954, 1958, 1961, 1970–71 and 1975. In the 1980s, consistently weak performance is observed in the Midwest.

The IUR series for the South suggests that economic performance in this region was weak from 1952 to 1960, but then strong from the mid-1960s through 1981. A weakening of the southern labor markets in the mid-1980s is also apparent.[4] In the West, strong performance

Table 5.4
Indices of Regional Labor Market Performance, 1948–1987

Year	North East			Midwest			South			West		
	IUR	TUR	Emp.	IUR	TUR	Emp.	IUR	TUR	Emp.	IUR	TUR	Emp.
1948	1.02	NA	1.00	0.75+	NA	1.02	0.91	NA	0.97+	1.40*	NA	0.99
1949	1.02	NA	1.00	0.82+	NA	1.02	0.97	NA	0.97+	1.15*	NA	1.00
1950	1.00	NA	1.00	0.83+	NA	1.01	1.04	NA	0.98	1.16*	NA	1.02
1951	1.07	NA	1.01	0.82+	NA	1.00	1.08	NA	0.98	0.96	NA	1.02
1952	1.03	NA	1.01	0.84+	NA	1.00	1.11*	NA	0.98	0.97	NA	1.01
1953	0.98	NA	1.01	0.79+	NA	0.99	1.23*	NA	1.00	1.07	NA	1.02
1954	0.94	NA	1.00	1.02	NA	0.99	1.21*	NA	1.00	0.78+	NA	1.01
1955	1.04	NA	1.01	0.86+	NA	0.99	1.20*	NA	1.00	0.84+	NA	1.01
1956	0.99	NA	1.00	1.00	NA	0.99	1.14*	NA	1.00	0.79+	NA	1.00
1957	1.00	NA	1.00	0.93	NA	1.00	1.14*	NA	1.01	0.88+	NA	1.00
1958	0.97	NA	0.99	1.11*	NA	1.02	1.04	NA	1.00	0.80+	NA	0.97+
1959	1.07	NA	1.00	0.89+	NA	1.01	1.14*	NA	1.01	0.82+	NA	0.97+
1960	0.98	NA	0.99	0.95	NA	1.01	1.11*	NA	1.02	0.94	NA	0.97+
1961	0.94	NA	0.98	1.03	NA	1.02	1.09	NA	1.02	0.92	NA	0.96+
1962	0.99	NA	0.98	0.93	NA	1.02	1.07	NA	1.02	0.98	NA	0.96+
1963	1.06	NA	0.99	0.86+	NA	1.01	1.00	NA	1.02	1.04	NA	0.97+
1964	1.05	NA	0.99	0.82+	NA	1.01	0.96	NA	1.02	1.17*	NA	0.98
1965	1.01	NA	0.99	0.75+	NA	0.99	0.92	NA	1.02	1.39*	NA	1.00
1966	1.04	NA	0.99	0.74+	NA	0.98	0.90+	NA	1.02	1.39*	NA	1.01
1967	0.96	0.92	0.99	0.85+	0.86+	0.98	0.93	1.09	1.02	1.34*	1.33*	1.02
1968	0.99	0.89+	0.99	0.86+	0.82+	0.98	0.92	1.09	1.02	1.29*	1.25*	1.02
1969	1.02	0.92	0.99	0.82+	0.82+	0.98	0.90+	1.09	1.02	1.32*	1.28*	1.02
1970	0.95	0.94	0.98	1.01	0.91	0.98	0.84+	1.00	1.02	1.26*	1.29*	1.03*
1971	1.04	1.05	0.99	1.00	0.92	0.99	0.79+	0.88+	1.00	1.18*	1.26*	1.04*

1972	1.18*	1.13*	1.00	0.95	0.88+	0.99	0.72+	0.91	0.99	1.16*	1.16*	1.04*
1973	1.22*	1.13*	1.02	0.87+	0.89+	0.98	0.72+	0.89+	0.98	1.21*	1.21*	1.03*
1974	1.16*	1.09	1.03*	0.97	0.85+	0.98	0.79+	0.97	0.98	1.10*	1.11*	1.03*
1975	1.05	1.12*	1.03*	1.06	0.92	0.98	0.99	0.96	0.99	0.90+	0.99	1.01
1976	1.12*	1.23*	1.04*	1.01	0.85+	0.97+	0.90+	0.94	0.99	1.00	1.04	1.01
1977	1.14*	1.19*	1.04*	1.00	0.84+	0.97+	0.89+	0.96	1.00	0.99	1.01	1.00
1978	1.15*	1.14*	1.05*	1.03	0.86+	0.97+	0.87+	0.98	1.00	0.97	0.99	0.99
1979	1.10*	1.14*	1.05*	1.15*	0.94	0.98	0.88+	0.99	1.00	0.88+	0.95	0.97+
1980	0.91	1.00	1.03*	1.45*	1.14*	1.00	0.87+	0.96	0.99	0.84+	0.89+	0.97+
1981	0.91	0.98	1.02	1.34*	1.12*	1.02	0.89+	0.98	0.98	0.94	0.89+	0.98
1982	0.84+	0.93	1.00	1.32*	1.13*	1.03*	0.97	0.98	0.98	0.96	0.93	0.99
1983	0.87+	0.91	0.99	1.20*	1.11*	1.04*	0.99	1.03	0.99	1.02	0.91	0.99
1984	0.93	0.91	0.98	1.15*	1.11*	1.03*	0.94	1.02	0.99	1.04	0.93	0.99
1985	0.88+	0.86+	0.97+	1.17*	1.10*	1.03*	0.95	1.06	1.00	1.07	0.93	1.00
1986	0.80+	0.80+	0.96+	1.13*	1.03	1.03*	1.06	1.16*	1.01	1.07	0.93	1.00
1987	0.78+	0.73+	0.95+	1.18*	1.07	1.02	1.03	1.17*	1.02	1.07	0.93	1.01

SOURCE: All indices based on regression equations from table 5.3. The IUR and TUR indices are ratios of actual unemployment rates to fitted rates from the regressions. The employment indices are ratios of fitted employment shares to actual shares. For all indices high ratios indicate years of poor regional labor market performance. Years with especially weak performance have *'s, and years with especially strong performance have +'s. NA = not available.

is observed from 1954 to 1961, but then weak performance prevailed from 1964 to 1974.

The labor market performance indices of table 5.4 are closely linked to the regional pattern of UI loans previously examined in table 5.1. Weak performance in the North East in the 1970s, in the Midwest throughout the 1980s, and in the South in the mid-1980s coincides with the timing of large-scale borrowing by states in each of these regions.

Weak performance in years prior to the mid-1970s was observed both in the South (from 1952 to 1960) and in the West (from 1964 to 1974). For these regions, however, the period of weak economic performance was not accompanied by large scale UI borrowing activity. Borrowing did not take place in the earlier periods for two reasons: trust fund reserves were more adequate and the average unemployment rates were lower (particularly in the West between 1964 and 1974). Regional reserve ratios at the start of the periods of weak labor market performance illustrate the long-term change in reserve adequacy over the 1948–1987 period. The four relevant reserve ratios (reserves as a percent of covered payrolls) were as follows: the South in 1952—7.0 percent;, the West in 1964—3.0 percent; the North East in 1972—2.4 percent; and the Midwest in 1980—.7 percent. Since reserve ratios are not likely to return to their levels of the 1950s, it seems likely that weak regional performance in the future will pinpoint the geographic areas where the need for UI loans will be the greatest.[5]

Another point is worth emphasizing in reference to the regional labor market performance. If a region experiences weak performance, UI claims rise due to higher unemployment. Weak performance, however, also affects revenues because employment growth is reduced. In table 5.4 especially weak employment growth is indicated between 1974 and 1980 in the North East, between 1982 and 1986 in the Midwest, and between 1970 and 1974 in the West. Financing problems are exacerbated by slow employment growth, which occurs in periods of weak economic performance.

Covariation Among State Unemployment Rates

The patterns of UI loan activities summarized earlier strongly suggest that individual states within larger geographic areas share similar unemployment experiences. This issue can be directly examined in a regression analysis of state unemployment rates.

As noted above, unemployment rates by geographic area are available from the CPS starting in 1967. In that year, annual unemployment rates were first published for the four census regions, the nine census divisions and the ten largest states. Later, the number of states expanded to 27 (in 1970) and then to 29 (in 1973), and finally to all states in 1976. Thus for the 1967–1987 period there are 810 state-year observations on annual state unemployment rates (TURs). These were the dependent variables in the regression analysis.

Three regression equations were tested to explain variation in state TURs. The regressions differed in the choice of the larger geographic areas used to explain individual state TURs, i.e., national, regional or divisional TURs. To the extent that state TURs are most similar to the TURs of adjacent states, then a clear ranking of the goodness-of-fit of the three regressions should be observed. The fit should be worst using the national TUR, intermediate using the regional TUR, and best using the divisional TUR. To reduce spurious correlation in the regressions, each state's unemployment was removed from the unemployment measure for the larger geographic area which included the state. For example, the three explanatory variables for the New York TUR observations were respectively TURs for the U.S. less New York, the North East region less New York, and the Mid-Atlantic division less New York.

Table 5.5 displays the regression results. All three regressions have positive slope coefficients indicating that state TURs increase when the TURs for the larger geographic areas increase. Observe that the R^2 is highest ($=.559$) when the explanatory variable is the TUR for the other states in the same census division, more than 20 percentage points higher than when the regional or national TUR is used. Note, however, that a large share of the variation in state TURs remains unexplained even in the best fitting equation. The TURs of states within census divisions are closely related, but do not move in perfect lock step.

Table 5.5
Simple Regressions Explaining State TURs
1967 to 1987

Constant	0.382	1.173	0.703
	(1.2)	(4.3)	(3.6)
U.S. TUR	0.913		
	(20.3)		
Regional TUR		0.806	
		(21.1)	
Divisional TUR			0.906
			(32.0)
Summary measures			
Number of observations	810	810	810
R^2	0.337	0.354	0.559
Standard error	1.855	1.831	1.514

SOURCE: All regressions use state TURs as the dependent variable. Independent variables are unemployment rates for the indicated geographic area after removal of the state's unemployment from the area's unemployment. All unemployment data from the Current Population Survey (CPS).

To further illustrate the similarity of unemployment rates in adjacent states, table 5.6 presents TURs for individual states in the North East region between 1970 and 1988. Data are available for five states for all years and for the four smaller New England states since 1976. Also shown are the national TUR and the TUR for the North East region. Relative unemployment rates (state rates divided by the national rate) appear in the bottom half of the table.

At least four observations should be made regarding the unemployment patterns in table 5.6. (1) Relative unemployment rates in the 1970s peaked earlier in New England states than in Mid-Atlantic states. For states with annual data extending back to 1970, relative unemployment rates of 1.20 and above are observed for the following consecutive sequences of years: 1971–1973 in Connecticut, 1973–1976 in Massachusetts, 1976–1979 in New York, and 1975–1977 in New Jersey.

(2) Low unemployment is pervasive throughout New England in the 1980s, especially in the later years of the decade. With only two exceptions (Maine in 1984 and 1986), relative unemployment rates of .75 or less are observed in all six states since 1984, and even earlier in New Hampshire (1978), Vermont (1981), and Connecticut (1982).

(3) Relative unemployment rates in some states deviate from relative rates in adjacent states for several consecutive years. Since 1976, New Hampshire generally has had the lowest rate while Maine has had either the highest or second highest rate among the six New England states. Since 1980, Pennsylvania has had the highest unemployment rate among the Mid-Atlantic states.

(4) The patterns of unusually high and unusually low state unemployment rates are closely linked to UI borrowing. Note the high unemployment in Connecticut starting in 1971 (while borrowing commenced in 1972). Low unemployment in New Hampshire helps explain why that state (alone among the nine states of the North East) did not need loans in the 1970s. The high unemployment in Pennsylvania in the 1980s helps explain why it was the only northeastern state to be a major borrower in the present decade.

Three implications of the preceding state and regional analysis may warrant some additional comments. The first relates to the geographic

Table 5.6
Unemployment Rates in the North East, 1970 to 1988

	Mass.	Conn.	Maine	N.H.	Vt.	R.I.	N.Y.	N.J.	Penn.	N. East	U.S.
	Annual unemployment rates										
1970	4.6	5.7		4.2[a]			4.5	4.6	4.5	4.6	4.9
1971	6.6	8.4		5.9[a]			6.6	5.7	5.4	6.2	5.9
1972	6.4	8.6		6.0[a]			6.7	5.8	5.4	6.2	5.6
1973	6.7	6.3		4.2[a]			5.4	5.6	4.8	5.5	4.9
1974	7.2	6.1		6.3[a]			6.4	6.3	5.1	6.1	5.6
1975	11.2	9.1		9.3[a]			9.5	10.2	8.3	9.5	8.5
1976	9.5	9.5	8.9	6.4	8.7	8.1	10.3	10.4	7.9	9.4	7.7
1977	8.1	7.0	8.4	5.9	7.0	8.6	9.1	9.4	7.7	8.4	7.1
1978	6.1	5.3	6.2	3.8	5.9	6.6	7.7	7.2	6.9	6.9	6.1
1979	5.5	5.1	7.2	3.1	5.1	6.6	7.1	6.9	6.9	6.6	5.8
1980	5.6	5.9	7.8	4.7	6.4	7.2	7.5	7.2	7.8	7.1	7.1
1981	6.4	6.2	7.2	5.0	5.7	7.6	7.6	7.3	8.4	7.4	7.6
1982	7.9	6.9	8.6	7.4	6.9	10.2	8.6	9.0	10.9	9.0	9.7
1983	6.9	6.0	9.0	5.4	6.9	8.3	8.6	7.8	11.8	8.7	9.6
1984	4.8	4.6	6.1	4.3	5.2	5.3	7.2	6.2	9.1	6.8	7.5
1985	3.9	4.9	5.4	3.9	4.8	4.9	6.5	5.7	8.0	6.2	7.2
1986	3.8	3.8	5.3	2.8	4.7	4.0	6.3	5.0	6.8	5.6	7.0
1987	3.2	3.3	4.4	2.5	3.6	3.8	4.9	4.0	5.7	4.5	6.2
1988	3.3	3.0	3.8	2.4	2.8	3.1	4.2	3.8	5.1	4.0	5.5
Averages											
1970–79	7.2	7.1		6.4[a]			7.3	7.2	6.3	6.9	6.2
1979–88	5.1	5.0	6.5	4.2	5.2	6.1	6.9	6.3	8.1	6.6	7.3

Relative unemployment rates

1970	0.94	1.16		0.86[a]		0.92	0.94	0.92	0.94	1.00
1971	1.12	1.42		1.00[a]		1.12	0.97	0.92	1.05	1.00
1972	1.14	1.54		1.07[a]		1.20	1.04	0.96	1.11	1.00
1973	1.37	1.29		0.86[a]		1.10	1.14	0.98	1.12	1.00
1974	1.29	1.09		1.12[a]		1.14	1.13	0.91	1.09	1.00
1975	1.32	1.07		1.09[a]		1.12	1.20	0.98	1.12	1.00
1976	1.23	1.23	1.16	0.83	1.05	1.34	1.35	1.03	1.22	1.00
1977	1.14	0.99	1.18	0.83	1.21	1.28	1.32	1.08	1.18	1.00
1978	1.00	0.87	1.02	0.62	1.08	1.26	1.18	1.13	1.13	1.00
1979	0.95	0.88	1.24	0.53	1.14	1.22	1.19	1.19	1.14	1.00
1980	0.79	0.83	1.10	0.66	1.01	1.06	1.01	1.10	1.00	1.00
1981	0.84	0.82	0.95	0.66	1.00	1.00	0.96	1.11	0.97	1.00
1982	0.81	0.71	0.89	0.76	1.05	0.89	0.93	1.12	0.93	1.00
1983	0.72	0.63	0.94	0.56	0.86	0.90	0.81	1.23	0.91	1.00
1984	0.64	0.61	0.81	0.57	0.71	0.96	0.83	1.21	0.91	1.00
1985	0.54	0.68	0.75	0.54	0.68	0.90	0.79	1.11	0.86	1.00
1986	0.54	0.54	0.76	0.40	0.57	0.90	0.71	0.97	0.80	1.00
1987	0.52	0.53	0.71	0.40	0.61	0.79	0.65	0.92	0.73	1.00
1988	0.60	0.55	0.69	0.44	0.56	0.76	0.69	0.93	0.73	1.00

SOURCE: All unemployment rate data based on the Current Population Survey and published in U.S. Department of Labor, *Geographic Profile of Employment and Unemployment*, various issues.

a. Average for four states for which individual state data are not available prior to 1976.

mobility of the labor force. Movement of workers between tight and loose labor markets is an important adjustment mechanism. Geographic mobility provides labor market rewards and helps to reduce unemployment rate differentials between geographic areas. The results of the table 5.5 regressions imply that unemployment differentials are smaller for adjacent states than for states that are farther apart. This suggests that, on average, the extra earnings and other economic rewards to migration will be larger for longer-distance moves. Also, since geographic mobility improves national labor market performance, national policies to promote mobility are to be encouraged.[6]

The second implication, directly related to UI financing, is that financing problems are apt to be experienced by adjacent states because high unemployment in one state is likely to be accompanied by high unemployment in surrounding states. The data examined in tables 5.1 and 5.6 support this strongly. Five of six New England states needed loans in the 1970s and borrowing equaled 2.89 percent of 1975 payrolls. In the 1980s, New England states borrowed only very small amounts (.14 percent of payrolls during 1980–1983 and .01 percent of payrolls during 1984–1987).

The third implication, also linked to UI financing, is that weak economic performance affects UI tax receipts as well as benefit outlays. Table 5.4 showed that weak unemployment performance in a region is associated with weak employment performance. Thus, when UI claims rise due to increased unemployment there is an associated tendency for employment growth to decline. This double-edged impact on UI trust funds is examined in the next section.

Financing Experiences in New Jersey

At the end of the 1980s, New Jersey was experiencing a prolonged economic expansion which began at the start of the decade. Unemployment in 1987 was only 4.0 percent of the labor force, 2.2 percentage points below the national average, and unemployment declined further to 3.8 percent in 1988. During the previous decade, however, the state's unemployment rate exceeded the national average in every year between 1972 and 1980. In 1975, when the national unemployment rate was 8.5 percent, New Jersey's was 10.2 percent, and the rate rose to 10.4 percent in the following year while national unemployment declined to 7.7 percent. (Recall the state and national rates in table 5.6.)

Thus during both the 1970s and 1980s, New Jersey had average unemployment rates that departed substantially from national unemployment rates. Between 1970 and 1979, the state's TUR averaged 7.2 percent, 1 percentage point above the national average. Between 1979 and 1988, however, the state's average TUR of 6.3 percent was 1 percentage point below the national average. The state was a major borrower in the 1970s (loans of $735 million during 1975–1978 equaled 3.27 percent of 1975 payrolls), but only a small-scale borrower in the 1980s (a 1983 loan of $78.5 million equaled .2 percent of 1981 payrolls).

When state unemployment departs from national unemployment, there are three separate effects on the UI trust fund balance.[7] Higher unemployment causes benefit outlays to increase and reduces the fund balance. Higher unemployment reduces covered employment and tax receipts and causes the fund balance to decline. Experience rating then operates to offset the former two effects and restore the fund balance to its previous level.

Simulations with the New Jersey model provide a way of estimating the size of the first two effects. These can be characterized respectively as the benefit effect and taxable wage effect of state unemployment deviations. In two simulations of the 1988–1997 period using respectively U.S. TURs from the 1970s and New Jersey TURs from the 1970s, the simulation based on the (higher) New Jersey TURs had $2.120 billion of higher benefit payments and $7 billion of lower taxable wages. Compared to the simulation using U.S. TURs, benefit payments were 16.8 percent higher and taxable wages were 1.6 percent lower. Of the two effects, the benefit effect accounted for 91.3 percent, and the taxable wage effect accounted for 8.7 percent of their combined adverse impact on the New Jersey trust fund.

When state versus national TURs from the 1980s (1979 to 1988) were used, similar qualitative results were obtained. In the simulation using (lower) New Jersey TURs, benefit payments were $2.003 billion (or 14.35 percent) lower, while taxable wages were $8 billion (or 1.85 percent) higher when compared to the simulation using the national TUR. Of the combined favorable effect on the trust fund, 88.6 percent was from lower benefits and 11.6 percent from higher taxable wages. Averaging the two sets of state versus national comparisons, about 90 percent of the combined effect on New Jersey trust fund flows was from changes in benefit payments, and about 10 percent was from changes in taxable wages. When the state TUR deviates from the national TUR, the effect on tax revenues is measurable but small compared to the effect on benefit outlays.

The simulation results can also be used to assess New Jersey's borrowing experiences of the 1970s. The "extra" state unemployment of the 1970s, i.e., the state TUR which averaged 7.2 percent less the U.S. TUR which averaged 6.2 percent, had an adverse impact on the trust fund of $2.322 billion in simulations covering the 1988–1997 period.[8] The $2.322 billion represents 2.35 percent of covered payroll for the middle year (1993) of the 10-year simulation. This scale of combined adverse benefit effect and taxable wage effect (their sum measured relative to covered payroll) is about three-quarters of the actual scale of state borrowing in the 1970s, i.e., 2.35 percent versus borrowing which equaled 3.27 percent of 1975 covered payroll. If New Jersey had experienced average unemployment during the 1970s, it certainly would have borrowed much less than $735 million, perhaps one-fourth of this amount.[9]

The effects of above-average unemployment on benefit payments and taxable wages have also been estimated in the other six states for which trust fund simulation models were developed (and previously used in chapter 4). The share of the combined effect accounted for by the taxable wage effect in New Jersey fell in the middle of the range for the seven states. In Ohio and Florida, only 6 percent of the combined effect of high unemployment was due to reductions in taxable wages, while 94 percent was due to increased benefits. The (reduced) taxable wage effects in the other states were as follows: Michigan—8 percent, Massachusetts and Texas—13 percent, and California—25 percent. Only in California did the taxable wage effect account for more than one-sixth of the combined effect. [10] In California, the higher taxable wage effect was attributable both to a smaller response of benefit outlays and a larger response of taxable wages to given increases in the average TUR. [11]

The models from the other states were also used to compare the scale of state borrowing in the 1970s and 1980s with the combined benefit effect and taxable wage effect of unusually high state unemployment. All simulations covered the 1988–1997 period, and the combined (benefit and taxable wage) effect over the 10 years was measured relative to total payrolls as of 1993, a mid-year of the simulations. In Massachusetts, the high average unemployment of the 1970s had a 10-year combined effect equal to 1.87 percent (of 1993 payrolls) compared to state borrowing in the 1970s which equaled 1.62 percent of 1975 payrolls. The simulated adverse effects of high unemployment in Michigan in the 1970s and 1980s were 3.73 percent and 7.57 percent (of 1993 payrolls) respectively. The scale of state borrowing in the 1970s was 2.29 percent of 1975 payrolls, and in the 1980s it was 6.67 percent of 1984 payrolls. For Ohio in the 1980s, the 10-year combined adverse benefit effect and taxable wage effect on the trust fund was 3.76 percent (of 1993 payrolls) compared to state borrowing which equaled 6.06 percent of 1984 payrolls.

This section has identified five instances where a state was a large-scale borrower: Massachusetts, Michigan, and New Jersey in the 1970s and Michigan and Ohio in the 1980s. In each of the five states, average TUR over 10 years exceeded the average U.S. TUR by at least 1.0 percentage point. Ten-year simulations then estimated the combined adverse effects of high unemployment on benefit payments and taxable wages in the states. In all five instances, the simulated effects of high state TURs represented at least 60 percent of the state's actual borrowing, and in three instances the size of the adverse effects exceeded the scale of state borrowing (Massachusetts and Michigan in the 1970s and Michigan in the 1980s). [12] Since individual states have little or no control over their own unemployment, the scale of their borrowing was at least partly due to adverse economic factors beyond their control.

NOTES

1. Throughout this chapter, geographic areas are identified using standard U.S. Bureau of the Census classifications, which divide the states into nine divisions. Table 5.1 adds Puerto Rico and the Virgin Islands to the Mid-Atlantic division. New England has six states: Connecticut, Maine, Massachusetts, New Hampshire, Rhode Island, and Vermont. The Mid-Atlantic states are New Jersey, New York, and Pennsylvania (plus Puerto Rico and the Virgin Islands for the analysis of loans). See table C-1 of U.S. Department of Labor (1988a) for a complete listing of states by census division. The divisions of the other simulation model states are as follows: East North Central (Ohio and Michigan), South Atlantic (Florida), West South Central (Texas), and Pacific (California).

2. The North East is defined as the states of the New England and Mid-Atlantic divisions. The Midwest consists of the states in the East North Central and West North Central divisions. The South combines the South Atlantic, East South Central, and West South Central divisions. The West region combines the states of the Mountain and Pacific divisions.

3. The same general pattern of regional coefficients was obtained in IUR regressions fitted to the 1967–1987 period. For the four regions, the slope coefficients were respectively 1.193, .988, .747 and 1.188. Thus a high-to-low ranking of UI benefit availability across the four regions would be as follows: North East, West, Midwest and South.

4. We know from data by census division that the weakening was pronounced in the West South Central division.

5. At the end of 1987, for example, the aggregate reserve ratio for the U.S. was 1.38 percent. For three earlier prerecession years aggregate reserve ratios were as follows: 1948—7.91 percent; 1959—3.57 percent; and 1969—3.46 percent.

6. Recent evidence from the UI Reemployment Demonstration Project in New Jersey, however, suggests that few claimants (less than 1 percent) avail themselves of relocation assistance (payments for out-of-area job interviews and payments for moving expenses)1. See part 2, section VI of Corson et al. (1989).

7. There is also an effect on interest income to the trust fund, which will be omitted from the present discussion.

8. This amount is the sum of $2.120 billion in additional benefit outlays and $.202 billion in reduced tax receipts due to lower taxable wages.

9. Since we are using a simulation over the 1988–1997 period to interpret events of the 1970s, the simulation results should be viewed as suggestive. A more precise quantitative estimate would have to hold constant other effects from the 1970s.

10. In each of the seven states, the share of the combined effect of high unemployment on the trust fund balance due to reduced taxable wages was estimated taking an average across four simulations. In each, deviations from the baseline simulation were noted. The four simulations used state and national TURs from the 1970s (1970–1979) and the 1980s (1979–1988). The average taxable wage effect shares in the seven states were as follows: Florida—.0552; Ohio—.0559; Michigan—.0800; New Jersey—.1084; Texas—.1255; Massachusetts—.1304; and California—.2486.

11. The smaller benefit response in California is due in part to its low weekly benefit amount. The larger taxable wage response is a partial reflection of a large covered employment response.
12. Recall the qualification noted in footnote 9. These comparisons are meant to be suggestive. The simulations did not try to hold constant other factors from the 1970s and 1980s besides state TURs, which could have affected borrowing in the individual states.

6
Federal Policies
to Encourage Solvency

In the mid- and late-1980s, state UI programs accumulated substantial reserve balances. At the end of 1989, aggregate net balances across all 53 programs totaled $36.9 billion or 1.90 percent of covered payrolls. The 1988 aggregate reserve ratio of 1.90 percent was considerably larger than the reserve ratio that existed at the start of the decade (.91 percent on January 1, 1980) but much smaller than the ratio at the start of the 1970s (3.46 percent). Despite this recent accumulation of reserves, many states remain exposed to the threat of insolvency. If the past is prologue, the next recession will be more severe in some geographic areas than others, and programs in the hardest hit regions will account for a major share of future UI loans.

Since large-scale borrowing remains a realistic possibility, it may be worthwhile to speculate on how the UI programs would respond to a future recession and how the response might be affected by federal policy initiatives regarding trust fund solvency. The discussion will emphasize how federal policy can affect trust fund balances, tax responsiveness, the terms and conditions for UI loans, and/or the possible supplementation of state fund balances in recognition of unusual needs.

The framework for the discussion is based on the earlier analysis of state funding strategies (chapter 2), but expanded to also consider possible interstate financial arrangements. The discussion will focus on how alternative federal policy stances can influence the states' choices of funding strategies. Recall that three funding strategies were identified in chapter 2: pre-funding, automatic pay-as-you-go, and discretionary pay-as-you-go.

Under the present federal policy stance regarding UI financing, the responsibility for financing benefit payments and making the associated decisions about appropriate trust fund balances is located at the state level. States are responsible for funding their own programs, using any combination of funding strategies. Alternatively, federal policy could be directed to actively encourage the states to do one of the following: (1) achieve a trust fund solvency standard; (2) include more flexible financing provisions in their laws; or (3) participate in a cost sharing/cost reimbursement arrangement whereby reserves from prosperous states are made available to those with "excess" costs (however defined).

The current federal policy stance towards state funding strategies might be characterized as one of *laissez faire*. States have exclusive responsibility for funding their own programs, with access to interest-bearing loans from the U.S. Treasury if they become insolvent. If a state borrows, it must repay the loan. Individual states are free to choose the relative degree of reliance to place on the three funding strategies.

Given events of 1980–1984 (the recessions, followed by state borrowing activities and UI legislative responses in the debtor states), the response by the states to a recession under the current federal policy regime can be suggested. A serious recession in 1990 or 1991 would cause several states to need UI loans. Likely candidates for borrowing would be states whose reserve ratio multiples were less than .5, e.g., Illinois, Louisiana, Michigan, Minnesota, Ohio, Pennsylvania, and Texas, to name seven with extensive borrowing histories from earlier in the 1980s.[1] The regional pattern of the recession would also influence which states would become large-scale borrowers. Major borrowers, in turn, would want to reduce and eliminate interest-bearing loans quickly. (Recall the repayment patterns identified previously in tables 1.4 and 1.5.) To eliminate their indebtedness, these states would be expected to enact solvency legislation (while still in the recession) that included both benefit reductions and tax increases.

The preceding stylized series of events has one very perverse outcome. States with serious unemployment problems find themselves under financial pressures to reduce benefits at a time when worker needs for benefits are unusually high. These pressures are strongest in states where initial trust fund reserve ratios are the lowest and where unemployment rates are the highest. Since fund balances at the end of the 1980s are more adequate than at start of the decade, the scale of state borrowing would likely be smaller than during the early 1980s.

For UI programs to be effective in meeting their micro (family level) and macro (automatic stabilizing) income maintenance objectives, benefit reductions should not occur in the midst of a recession. The alternative federal policy stances to be discussed below could modify this undesirable outcome.

Even if the federal government were not to modify its present *laissez-faire* policy stance, it might take actions that would affect the risk of insolvency in the states. To the extent that macroeconomic monetary and fiscal policies continue to achieve and maintain full employment, this will prevent the major increases in benefit payments that are the proximate cause for state solvency problems. Also, federal legislation to raise the taxable wage base for the Federal Unemployment Tax would cause many states to raise their own tax bases. The resulting increase in revenues would enhance trust fund balances in states that currently maintain the minimum permissible state taxable wage base, i.e., $7,000 per covered worker. Both federal actions would affect trust fund balances without trying to actively influence state choices of funding strategies. Other federal actions could affect state choices.

Pre-Funding

Active federal pursuit of a UI trust fund solvency standard could raise fund balances and reduce the anticipated scale of future borrowing. Federal policy could be implemented via a regulatory approach or an approach that emphasized financial incentives. The regulatory approach could specify a solvency standard, e.g., a reserve ratio (or high cost) multiple of 1.5 or 1.0, which was a conformity requirement.[2]

Alternatively, there could be a suggested federal solvency standard (not a conformity requirement) coupled with a federal policy that provided financial rewards and financial penalties dependent upon achievement of the standard. The financial reward could take the form of a federal interest rate supplementation for large reserve balances, e.g., the U.S. Treasury could add, say, 1 percentage point to the interest rate paid on state trust fund balances. An example might be as follows:

a suggested reserve ratio multiple of 1.0 with interest rate supplementation for balances in the range of reserve multiples of from .5 to 1.0. This would encourage the states to achieve a reserve ratio multiple of 1.0, but only cause extra interest costs for the U.S. Treasury on a fraction of the implied level of reserves and no extra interest costs on reserves that exceed the suggested standard. A rough calculation for 1988 suggests that the maximum cost of this specific policy would be $2.0 billion or .11 percent of covered payrolls.[3] The financial penalty for not achieving the standard could be assessed on the interest rate charged to states needing UI loans. The combined effects of extra interest for larger balances plus lower interest charges on loans could be a powerful stimulant for state trust fund accumulations.

Many other variants of the preceding financial incentives could be proposed. Since we know that even with a reserve ratio multiple of 1.5 UI loans are a distinct possibility (recall chapter 4), there still would be some borrowing in recessions. With higher initial balances, however, the volume of required loans would be reduced. There would be rewards to states for prudent fiscal behavior both before recessions and during recessions. With less need for loans in recessions, the tendency to reduce benefits in recessions would also be lessened.

Flexible Financing

Federal policy could encourage states to adopt financing arrangements which increased the cyclical responsiveness of UI taxes and, perhaps, of UI benefits as well. Achievement of flexible financing arrangements would enhance a state's reliance on the automatic pay-as-you-go funding strategy. There is definite state interest in flexible financing, as well as recent examples of legislation designed to achieve increased flexibility.[4] Flexible financing provisions were central to the laws enacted in Illinois in 1987 and in Pennsylvania in 1988. In these two states the new laws increased both revenue flexibility and benefit flexibility.[5] Pennsylvania's new law increased flexibility through variable surtaxes on employers, variable employee taxes, and variability in the weekly benefit amount. Automatic tax increases and benefit reductions occur when the state's trust fund balance falls below predetermined thresholds.[6] Proponents of flexible financing arrangements argue that they allow a state to operate with a lower average trust fund balance over the business cycle when compared to states that pre-fund against future contingencies. One possible advantage of the lower balance is that it helps prevent benefit liberalizations (induced by higher trust fund balances).

Three arguments against flexible funding arrangements were noted previously in chapter 2. (1) They may not operate on a large enough scale to prevent insolvency in serious recessions. (2) Because employer profits drop sharply in recessions, they impose tax increases at a time when profits are already low. States such as Texas and Louisiana were not willing to let their automatic tax increases go into effect in 1983 and 1984 because they implied such large changes in employer taxes.[7] (3) To the extent that flexible financing extends to UI benefits, it means that benefits (for at least some recipients) are reduced during recessions. Thus, increased burdens on both employers and UI recipients are imposed at an inappropriate point in the business cycle, i.e., when unemployment is high.

For the seven states examined in chapter 4, evidence from the simulations suggested that automatic solvency taxes did not operate on a sufficient scale to prevent large-scale borrowing in serious recessions. If this conclusion holds generally for states with solvency taxes and other automatic pay-as-you- go provisions, there would seem to be a paradox. Flexible financing arrangements with small effects on taxes and benefits might be allowed to be fully operative in a recession, but they would not prevent insolvency. On the other hand, provisions with larger-scale effects might not be allowed to operate, e.g., the experiences of Texas and Louisiana in 1982–1984. The net effect of reliance on flexible financing could be twofold: (1) keeping pre-recession fund balances smaller than they otherwise would be, and (2) not preventing insolvency in serious recessions. In effect, flexible financing would be like an umbrella that protected against light rain showers but not against thunderstorms.

Proponents of flexible financing arrangements would undoubtedly downplay the practical importance of the preceding considerations. At present, states can modify their laws to achieve increased flexibility without the need for federal policy actions. If federal policy wanted to actively encourage flexible funding arrangements this could be accomplished by mandating new conformity requirements. In effect, federal laws could be structured to force changes in existing tax and benefit statutes in the states. Regarding state tax statutes, there could be requirements mandating: (1) short delays between changes in trust fund balances and changes in employer taxes; (2) wide minimum ranges of experience rated tax rates; and (3) (in benefit ratio states) short experience periods for measuring employer benefit ratios, i.e., less than the three years presently used in most benefit ratio states. Since the potential financial penalties are large for states that do not satisfy conformity requirements (the loss of the ability to reduce state tax rates below 5.4 percent through experience rating), federal policy could strongly encourage increased state reliance on flexible financing. It is not obvious that such a federal policy would be prudent or who might advocate such a federal policy stance.

Cost Reinsurance and Cost Equalization

Unlike the present situation where each state is responsible for financing its own benefits, cost reinsurance and cost equalization promote the sharing of UI costs across states.[8] Proponents argue that certain states should be eligible for financial assistance because of unusually bad economic circumstances, circumstances unexpected and beyond their control.

Cost reinsurance in UI is modeled after cost reinsurance in other areas of private insurance. A group of insurers (states) pays into a common fund and those with unusually bad experiences receive payments from the common fund to cover part or all of the excess costs due to unforeseeable events. Cost reinsurance in UI typically uses past benefit cost experiences to gauge expected experiences, and identifies as eligible reimbursable costs those substantially above expected costs. Each state's own past experience is used to determine its eligibility for reinsurance payments from the common pool to the state trust fund.

Under cost equalization, states that experience costs (or unemployment rates) in excess of an absolute threshold would have some (or all) of their excess costs covered by payments from the U.S. Treasury or from a cost equalization fund. A major justification for cost equalization is to relieve states from excessive cost burdens that have arisen from economic factors beyond state control.

Cost reinsurance and cost equalization expand the scope of responsibility for covering individual states' UI costs. Those states with unusually strong economic performance assume part of the responsibility for benefit payments made in states experiencing unusually weak performance. Two premises of these proposals are that individual states and regions can experience economic fortunes which depart substantially from the national experience and that such departures can persist for several consecutive years. The analysis of chapter 5 showed that substantial and persistent state and regional departures have taken place in the U.S. since World War II and that downward deviations adversely affect UI tax revenues as well as benefit payments. Since the states and regions have not been the principal cause for the deviations, a case can be advanced for having the states with stronger performance help the weaker ones. A major question for these arrangements is how much cross-subsidization there should be.

Under the present system of UI financing, each state generates the tax revenues that pay for program benefits. The presence of U.S. Treasury loans does not change the full responsibility of each state for financing its own benefits. Loans merely change the timing of when state taxes are paid. Under cost reinsurance and cost equalization, exclusive state responsibility for UI financing no longer holds. However, the operation of either type of cost sharing plan does not necessarily imply that some states will always be net recipients while others will always be net donors. The chapter 5 analysis of state and regional labor market performance since World War II documented large-scale changes in the relative economic fortunes of the major census regions. Over a period of several decades, the extent of the net interregional subsidies would undoubtedly be much smaller than for shorter, say, 10-year, periods.[9]

Specific proposals for cost reinsurance and cost equalization were made at various times in the 1950s, 1960s, and 1970s, but they have not been actively pursued in the decade of the 1980s.[10] Many important details need to be considered. Crosslin (1980), for example, discusses four important considerations: (1) individual state eligibility criteria; (2) the definition of "normal" benefit costs needed to identify excessive costs; (3) the amount of a state's grant, i.e., the parameters of the excess cost reimbursement schedule; and (4) the source of funding. Although many specific questions would need to be addressed by a particular cost reinsurance or cost equalization plan, the main principle is simple, i.e., shared (interstate) responsibility for funding excess costs incurred by the states experiencing the worst economic conditions.

One important advantage of cost sharing and cost reinsurance arrangements is that the UI system needs smaller aggregate reserves than when each state is exclusively responsible for its own costs. Resources can flow across state lines to UI programs in regions of excessive UI costs. To function successfully, a system of cost sharing must have a sufficient amount of initial reserves so that there exists an ample stock of reserves to be shared. This condition is more fully satisfied in the late 1980s than it was at the start of the decade.

Federal policy can directly promote cost reinsurance or cost equalization through legislation. No plans have been proposed since the late 1970s. Considering the higher levels of reserves achieved by states in the late 1980s and the likelihood of continuing future changes in regional economic fortunes, now may be a good time to renew active consideration of cost reinsurance and cost equalization plans.

In the late 1980s, some favorable conditions exist that may enhance the prospects of federal legislation to institute cost reinsurance or cost equalization. As a result of the recessions of the mid-1970s and early 1980s, nearly three-quarters of the UI programs (38 of 53) have borrowed at least once from the U.S. Treasury. These experiences may make a pooling arrangement more attractive to states than in the past.

Also, two federal trust funds, the Federal Unemployment Account (FUA) and the Extended Unemployment Compensation Account (EUCA), are slated to grow substantially by the early 1990s. With a history of borrowing and the existence of substantial state-financed federal accounts, a majority of states might be willing to contemplate using these accounts for state trust fund loans in a future recession. Demonstrated federal leadership would be needed to accomplish the required statutory changes.

The chapter has briefly examined how federal policy could influence state funding strategies. A continuation of the current federal policy stance is probably the most likely one to be followed in the near term. To guard against further recession-induced benefit reductions, however, a case can be made that federal policy should promote both state adherence to a solvency standard and a form of cost sharing or cost reinsurance among the states.

NOTES

1. The reserve ratio multiples were computed for these states as of the end of 1988.

2. To be allowed to use experience rating to reduce employer state UI tax rates below 5.4 percent of taxable payrolls, the solvency standard would have to be satisfied. For states that did not satisfy the requirement when the standard became effective, a timetable for achieving the solvency standard could also be specified.

3. The calculation was done as follows: covered wages of $1,798 billion, the high cost ratio (benefits as a percent of payroll) for the U.S. of 2.24 percent and extra interest of $2.0 billion.

4. Prior to its financing problems of the 1980s, UI officials from Texas had frequently argued in favor of flexible financing provisions of their tax statute.

5. The Illinois provisions were described earlier in chapter 2.

6. The trigger mechanism in Pennsylvania uses the ratio of the trust fund balances on July 1st to benefit payments over the preceding three years.

7. See the details for both states in chapter 2 of Vroman (1986).

8. See Becker (1980) and Crosslin (1980) for discussions of cost reinsurance and cost equalization.

9. The absence of long-term net interregional subsidies would be more likely if unemployment rates (especially TURs) rather than benefit cost rates (benefits as a percent of payrolls) were used to direct the net financial flows among the states. Use of benefit cost rates in a cost equalization plan would be more likely to work to the disadvantage of low-cost states.

10. Becker (1980, p. 350) discusses aspects of the Loyson reinsurance plan that strongly influenced an ICESA catastrophic reinsurance proposal of 1963. He also discusses a Broadhead-Javits plan of the late 1970s.

Appendix A
The Massachusetts Model

All variables used in the model of Massachusetts are defined in this appendix. Also shown are the behavioral equations and definitional relations that link the model's variables.

BLOCK 1
LABOR MARKET

GRCLF	Growth rate in the labor force, percent	Exogenous variable
GRAWW	Growth rate in average weekly wages, percent	Exogenous variable
INTRAT	Interest rate on trust fund balances, percent	Exogenous variable
TUR	Total unemployment rate, percent	Exogenous variable
CLF	Labor force	$= (1 + \text{GRCLF}/100) * \text{CLF}_{-1}$
TU	Total unemployment	$= \text{CLF} * \text{TUR}/100$
ECPS	Total employment	$= \text{CLF} - \text{TU}$

ETX — Employment of taxable covered employers

$$= -669.259 + .991*\text{ECPS} + 94.812*\text{D78}$$
$$\quad\ \ (1.7) \quad\cdot\ \ (6.7) \qquad\qquad (2.3)$$
$$+ 44.798*\text{D85} + .812*\text{RHO}$$
$$\quad (1.3) \qquad\qquad (5.6)$$

$\bar{R}^2 = .986$ S.E. $= 32.19$ D.W. $= 1.20$
Sample period 1968 to 1987
D78 $= 1$ from 1978 to 1987, $= 0$ otherwise
D85 $= 1$ from 1985 to 1987, $= 0$ otherwise
Model intercept $= -629.259$ to adjust for average residuals in 1986 and 1987

EREI — Employment of reimbursable covered employers

$$= 458 + .05*(\text{ETX} - 2477)$$
EREI in 1987 $= 458$
ETX in 1987 $= 2477$

ECOV	Employment covered by the UI program	$= \text{ETX} + \text{EREI}$
AWW	Average weekly wages in covered employment	$= (1 + \text{GRAWW}/100) * \text{AWW}_{-1}$

BLOCK 2
BENEFITS

IU — Insured unemployment

$$= 30.355 + .5327*\text{TU} - .2073*\text{TU}_{-1}$$
$$\quad (8.2) \qquad (15.2) \qquad\quad (6.1)$$
$$- 7.302*\text{D81}$$
$$\quad (2.7)$$

$\bar{R}^2 = .947$ S.E. $= 5.72$ D.W. $= 1.51$
Sample period 1967 to 1987
D81 $= 1$ from 1981 to 1987, $= 0$ otherwise

153

IUR	Insured unemployment rate	$=100*IU/ECOV$

| IUTXIU | Ratio of IU of taxable employers to total IU | Exogenous variable, $= .964$, average for 1983-1987 |

| WBWCL | Ratio of weeks paid to weeks claimed | Exogenous variable, $= .897$, average for 1983-1987 |

| REPLRT | Replacement rate, ratio of weekly benefits to average weekly wages | $= .3841 + .00301*TUR - .00359*GRAWW$
$(36.7)\quad (3.2)\qquad\quad (2.6)$
$+ .0163*D85$
(2.8)
$\bar{R}^2 = .410\quad S.E. = .0083\quad D.W. = .96$
Sample period 1967 to 1987
D85 = 1 from 1985 to 1987, = 0 otherwise |

| WBAPRE | Weekly benefit amount, pre 1987 | $= REPLRT*AWW$ |

| WBA | Weekly benefit amount, 1987 and later years | $= WBAPRE + ADJ$
ADJ = \$5 in 1987, =\$8 in 1988 and later years |

| BENADJ | Benefit adjustment, adjusts product of benefit variables to agree with aggregate benefit payments in regular UI | Exogenous variable, $= .969$, average for 1983-1987 |

| BENREG | Aggregate benefit payments for the regular UI program | $= IU*IUTXIU*WBWCL*WBA*BENADJ*(.052)$ |

| EBON | Trigger to turn on the EB program | $= 1$ if $IUR \geq 3.98\%$, otherwise $= 0$ |

| MOEB03 | EB program triggered on for 3 months | $= 3$ if $4.69\% > IUR \geq 3.98\%$, otherwise $= 0$ |

| MOEB05 | EB program triggered on for 5 months | $= 5$ if $4.99\% > IUR \geq 4.7\%$, otherwise $= 0$ |

| MOEB08 | EB program triggered on for 8 months | $= 8$ if $5.29\% > IUR \geq 5.0\%$, otherwise $= 0$ |

| MOEB10 | EB program triggered on for 10 months | $= 10$ if $5.59\% > IUR \geq 5.3\%$, otherwise $= 0$ |

| MOEB12 | EB program triggered on for 12 months | $= 12$ if $IUR \geq 5.6\%$, otherwise $= 0$ |

| MOEB | Months EB program is triggered on for the year | $= MOEB03 + MOEB05 + MOEB08 + MOEB10 + MOEB12$ |

| APWKEB | Ratio of annualized weeks compensated in EB to weeks compensated in the regular UI program | $= .08115 + .0213*IURAV$
$(2.3)\quad (3.0)$
$\bar{R}^2 = .441\quad S.E. = .028\quad D.W. = 2.29$
$IURAV = (IUR + IUR_{-1})/2$
Sample period = 1971-78, 1980-82 |

| WBAEB | Weekly benefit amount for EB beneficiaries | $= .909*WBA$
$.909 = $ Av. (WBAEB/WBA) for 1980-1982 |

EBADJ	EB benefit adjustment, adjusts product of EB variables to agree with total EB payments	Exogenous variable, $-.8857$, average for 1980-1982
EBTOT	Total EB payments	$= (EBON - 1)*IU*IUTXIU*WBWCL*(MOEB/12)* APWKEB*WBAEB*EBADJ*(.052)$
EBS	State share of EB costs	$= EBTOT/2$
BEN	Total benefit payments from the trust fund	$= BENREG + EBS$

BLOCK 3
TAXES

TXBASE	Taxable wage base	Exogenous variable
TBAW	Ratio of the taxable wage base to average weekly wages	$= TXBASE/(52*AWW)$
TWP	Taxable wage proportion	$=(1.487*TBAW - .870*TBAW^2)*(1 - .00940*TUR)$ $\quad(41.5)\qquad\quad(14.3)\qquad\qquad\qquad(5.6)$ $\bar{R}^2 = .980$ S.E. $= .00793$ D.W. $= .97$ Sample period 1967 to 1987
RESNL	Net trust fund reserves at the end of last year	Predetermined variable
RES930	Net trust fund reserves on Sept. 30 of last year	$= .75*RESNL + .25*RESNL_{-1}$
RRLAG	Reserve ratio at the end the last calendar year	$= RESNL/WSTOL$ WSTOL = total wages and salaries of taxable employers, last year
RESTX	Net trust fund reserves from last year used to determine this year's applicable tax schedule	$= RES930 + .134*TAX_{-1}$ TAX = total tax payments
WSTS	Wages and salaries of taxable employers used to determine this year's applicable tax schedule	$= .911*WSTO_{-2}$ WSTOL = total wages and salaries of taxable employers, two year lag
RRTS	Reserve ratio used to determine this year's applicable tax schedule	$= RESTX/WSTS$
TXSCHA	Tax schedule A in effect	Predetermined variable, tax rate = 3.3%, in effect if RRTS $\geq$ 2.3%
TXSCHB	Tax schedule B in effect	Predetermined variable, tax rate = 3.6%, in effect if 2.3% > RRTS $\geq$ 2%
TXSCHC	Tax schedule C in effect	Predetermined variable, tax rate = 3.9%, in effect if 2% > RRTS $\geq$ 1.7%
TXSCHD	Tax schedule D in effect	Predetermined variable, tax rate = 4.2%, in effect if 1.7% > RRTS $\geq$ 1.4%
TXSCHE	Tax schedule E in effect	Predetermined variable, tax rate = 4.5%, in effect if 1.4% > RRTS $\geq$ 1.1%
TXSCHF	Tax schedule F in effect	Predetermined variable, tax rate = 4.8%, in effect if 1.1% > RRTS $\geq$ .8%

TXSCHG	Tax schedule G in effect	Predetermined variable, tax rate = 5.1%, in effect if .8% > RRTS
TRSTAT	Statutory tax rate in effect for the current year	Predetermined variable, average rate as shown for schedules A (3.3%) through G (5.1%)

ETRSCH	Effective tax rate on taxable wages determined from the tax rate schedule	= 1.2460 + .6391*TRSTAT - .8612*D78
		    (5.3) (11.6) (14.8)
		- .1511*(100*RRLAG)
		   (4.0)
		
		$\bar{R}^2$ = .981 S.E. = .103 D.W. = 1.92
		D78 = 1 from 1978 to 1987, =0 otherwise
		Sample period 1967 to 1987

NCHP1	Noncharged benefits proportion no. 1	= .1 if RRLAG ≥4%, otherwise = 0
NCHP2	Noncharged benefits proportion no. 2	= .1 +.02*(4 - RRLAG%) if 4% > RRLAG ≥2%, otherwise = 0
NCHP3	Noncharged benefits proportion no. 3	= .14 +.04*(2 - RRLAG%) if 2% > RRLAG ≥1% otherwise = 0
NCHP4	Noncharged benefits proportion no. 4	= .18 +.06*(1 -RRLAG%) if 1%> RRLAG ≥-.5% otherwise = 0
NCHP5	Noncharged benefits proportion no.5	= .27 if -.5% > RRLAG. otherwise = 0
NCHPRO	Noncharged benefits proproportion, proportion of BEN that is noncharged	= NCHP1 + NCHP2 + NCHP3 + NCHP4 + NCHP5
NONCHG	Noncharged benefits	= NCHPRO*BEN
SOLVAS	Solvency assessment	= (NONCHG - INT)$_{-1}$ INT = interest income for the year
TRSOLV	Tax rate for the Solvency tax	= 100*SOLVAS/WSTO Rounded to the nearest .01 WSTO = Total wages and salaries of taxable covered employers
ETR	Total effective tax rate on taxable covered employers	= ETRSCH + TRSOLV
WSTO	Total wages and salaries of taxable covered employers	= ETX*AWW*(.052)
TAX	Total tax payments	= WSTO*TWP*(ETR/100)

BLOCK 4
INTEREST

INTRT	Interest rate on trust fund balances	Exogenous variable
RESNL	Net trust fund reserves at the end of last year	Predetermined variable

RESNHT	Initial estimate of trust fund balance, end of current year	= RESNL + TAX - BEN
RESNAV	Average trust fund balance for the year	= (RESNL + RESNHT)/2
RESNPB	Average positive fund balance for the year	= RESNAV if RESNAV > 0, otherwise = 0
INT	Interest income for the year	= INTRT*RESNPB

BLOCK 5
FUND BALANCE

RESNL	Net trust fund reserves at the end of last year	Predetermined variable
TAX	Total tax payments	Endogenous variable, determined in Block 3
INT	Interest income for the year	Endogenous variable, determined in Block 4
BEN	Total benefit payments from the trust fund	Endogenous variable, determined in Block 2
RESNET	Net trust fund reserves at the end of the current year	= RESNL + TAX + INT - BEN

Appendix B
The Texas Model

All variables used in the model of Texas are defined in this appendix. Also shown are the behavioral equations and definitional relations that link the model's variables.

BLOCK 1
LABOR MARKET

| GRCLF | Growth rate in the labor force, percent | Exogenous variable |

| GRAWW | Growth rate in average weekly wages, percent | Exogenous variable |

| INTRAT | Interest rate on trust fund balances, percent | Exogenous variable |

| TUR | Total unemployment rate, percent of labor force | Exogenous variable |

CLF   Labor force $= (1 + GRCLF/100)*CLF_{-1}$

TU   Total unemployment $= CLF*TUR/100$

ECPS   Total employment $= CLF - TU$

PEMM   Proportion of employment in mining and manufacturing

$$= .2397 - .00498*TUR - .00491*TUR_{-1}$$
$$(15.2) \quad (3.3) \quad\quad (3.4)$$
$$+ .8175*RHO$$
$$(6.1)$$
$\bar{R}^2 = .858$ S.E. $= .00596$ D.W. $= 1.22$
Sample period 1968 to 1987

EMM   Employment in mining and manufacturing $= ECPS * PEMM$

ETAX   Employment of taxable covered employers

$$= -1234.350 + .6111*ECPS + 1.3833*EMM$$
$$(10.6) \quad (32.0) \quad\quad (12.3)$$
$$+ 277.511*D72 + 71.571*D78$$
$$(9.0) \quad\quad\quad (1.5)$$
$\bar{R}^2 = .999$ S.E. $= 37.31$ D.W. $= 2.05$
Sample period 1967 to 1987
D72 $= 1$ from 1972 to 1987, $= 0$ otherwise
D78 $= 1$ from 1978 to 1987, $= 0$ otherwise

EREI   Employment of reimbursable covered employers

$= EREI_{-1} + 28.7$
Ave. increase in EREI from 1979 to 1987
$= 28.7$. EREI in 1987 $= 976.$

ECOV   Employment covered by the UI program $= ETAX + EREI$

AWW   Average weekly wages in covered employment $= (1 + GRAWW/100)*AWW_{-1}$

AWWMFG   Average weekly wages in manufacturing

$$= 5.7377 + 1.0187*AWW$$
$$(1.6) \quad (87.1)$$
$\bar{R}^2 = .999$ S.E. $= 2.745$ D.W. $= 1.793$
Sample period 1976 to 1987

BLOCK 2
BENEFITS

IU   Insured unemployment

$$= - 14.232 + .302*TU - .052*TU_{-1}$$
$$(2.2) \quad\quad (8.4) \quad\quad (1.5)$$
$$-10.780*D81$$
$$(1.2)$$

$\bar{R} = .949$ S.E. $= 9.72$ D.W. $= 2.14$
Sample period 1967 to 1987
D81 = 1 from 1981 to 1987, = 0 otherwise

IUR   Insured unemployment rate

$= 100*IU/ECOV$

IUTXIU   Ratio of IU of taxable employers to total IU

Exogenous variable,
$= .970$, average for 1983-1987

WPDWCL   Ratio of weeks paid to weeks claimed

$$= .6269 + .03400*TUR$$
$$(19.3) \quad (5.9)$$

$\bar{R} = .628$ S.E. $= .0424$ D.W. $= .78$
Sample period 1967 to 1987

DAWWMFGL   Change in Mfg. average weekly wage, lagged

$= AWWMFG_{-1} - AWWMFG_{-2}$

CAROVER   Carryover of DAWWMFGL from last year

$= TOTINCR_{-1} - FULLTEN_{-1}$
(See below)

TOTINCR   Total increment in AWWMFG used to determine the increase in the maximum weekly benefit

$= DAWWMFGL + CAROVER$

FULLTEN   Full ten dollar increments in AWWMFG

$= TOTINCR$ rounded down to the nearest ten dollars

MAXWBA   Maximum weekly benefit amount

$= MAXWBA_{-1} + (.7*FULLTEN)$
(MAXWBA frozen in 1988 and 1989)

MBAWW   Ratio of maximum weekly benefit to average weekly wage

$= MWBA/AWW$

REPLRT   Replacement rate, ratio of weekly benefits to average weekly wages

$$= -.1006 + 1.5565*MBAW - 1.3752*MBAW^2$$
$$(1.1) \quad\quad (3.5) \quad\quad\quad\quad (2.4)$$
$$+ .00908*TUR - .00267*GRAWW$$
$$(4.6) \quad\quad\quad (3.1)$$

$\bar{R}^2 = .975$ S.E. $= .00739$ D.W. $= 2.41$
Sample period 1967 to 1987

WBA   Weekly benefit amount

$= REPLRT*AWW$

BENADJ   Benefit adjustment, adjusts product of benefit variables to agree with aggregate benefit payments in regular UI

Exogenous variable,
$= .969$, average for 1984-1987

BENREG   Aggregate benefit payments for the regular UI program

$= IU*IUTXIU*WPDWCL*WBA*BENADJ*(.052)$

EBON   Trigger to turn on the EB program

$= 1$ if IUR $\geq 3.98\%$, otherwise $= 0$

MOEBO3   EB program triggered on for 3 months

$= 3$ if $4.7\% >$ IUR $\geq 4.0\%$,
otherwise $= 0$

MOEB05	EB program triggered on for 5 months	= 5 if 5.0% > IUR ≥ 4.7%, otherwise = 0
MOEB08	EB program triggered on for 8 months	= 8 if 5.3% > IUR ≥ 5.0%, otherwise = 0
MOEB10	EB program triggered on for 10 months	= 10 if 5.62% > IUR ≥ 5.3%, otherwise = 0
MOEB12	EB program triggered on for 12 months	= 12 if IUR ≥5.62 %, otherwise = 0
MOEB	Months EB program is triggered on for the year	= MOEB03 + MOEB05 + MOEB08 + MOEB10 + MOEB12
PYEBON	Proportion of the year EB is "ON"	= MOEB/12

$$EBENPROP \quad \text{Extended benefits as a proportion of regular benefits} \quad = .2584*PYEBON$$
$$(27.5)$$

$$\bar{R}^2 = .977 \quad S.E. = .0155$$
Sample period 1972, 1975-78, 1980-81

EBTOT	Total EB payments	= (EBON - 1)*BENREG*EBENPROP
EBS	State share of EB costs	= EBTOT/2
BEN	Total benefit payments from the trust fund	= BENREG + EBS

BLOCK 3
TAXES

TXBASE	Taxable wage base	Exogenous variable
TBAW	Ratio of the taxable wage base to average weekly wages	= TXBASE/(52*AWW)

$$TWP \quad \text{Taxable wage proportion}$$
$$=(1.536*TBAW - .861*TBAW^2)*(1 - .00902*TUR$$
$$(54.2) \qquad (18.7) \qquad\qquad (4.0)$$
$$- .00726*TUR_{-1}$$
$$(3.6)$$

$$\bar{R}^2 = .996 \quad S.E. = .00372 \quad D.W. = 1.39$$
Sample period 1967 to 1987
Fitted by nonlinear least squares

WSTO	Total wages and salaries of taxable covered employers	= ETAX*AWW*(.052)
WSTX	Taxable wages and salaries of taxable covered employers	= WSTO*TWP
BENTAX	Benefits of taxable employers to be financed by employer taxes	= (.75*BEN_{-1}) + (.25*BEN_{-2})
PEFFCHG	Proportion of BENTAX effectively charged to taxable employers	Exogenous variable

EFFCHG	Effective charges	$= PEFFCHG*BENTAX$
INEFFCHG	Ineffective charges	$= BENTAX - EFFCHG$
EFFCHG3	Effective charges for the three years used in benefit ratio calculations	$= BENTAX + BENTAX_{-1} + BENTAX_{-2}$
WSTX630	Taxable wages and salaries for the year ending June 30th of last year	$= (.5*WSTX_{-1}) + (.5*WSTX_{-2})$
WSTX930	Taxable wages and salaries for the year ending Sept. 30th of last year	$= (.75*WSTX_{-1}) + (.25*WSTX_{-2})$
WSTX3	Taxable wages and salaries for the three years used in benefit ratio calculations	$= WSTX930 + WSTX930_{-1} + WSTX930_{-2}$
BRNRATIO	Benefit ratio used in employer tax calculations	$= 100*EFFCHG3/WSTX3$
RPLNRATO	Replenishment ratio	$= (EFFCHG + (.5*INEFFCHG))/EFFCHG$
TRBASRAW	Basic tax rate, raw calculation	$= BENRATIO*RPLNRATO$
TRBASIC	Basic tax rate, constrained	$= Minimum(TRBASRAW, 6\%)$
TRREPLEN	Tax rate for the replenishment tax	$= 100*(.5*INEFFCHG)/WSTX630$, rounded to the nearest .01
RES930	Net trust fund reserves on Sept. 30 of last year	$= (.75*RESNET_{-1}) + (.25*RESNET_{-2})$
RRWTX930	Reserve ratio on Sept 30 of last year, percent of taxable wages	$= 100*RES930/WSTX630$
DEFTAXON	Deficit tax on?	$= 1$ (yes) if $RRWTX930 <= 1.0$, otherwise $= 0$
CREDITON	Tax credit on?	$= 1$ (yes) if $RRWTX930 >= 2.0$, otherwise $= 0$
FLOOR	Trust fund floor for deficit tax	$= Maximum(400, .01*WSTX630)$
CEILING	Trust fund ceiling for receiving a tax credit	$= .02*WSTX630$
BASCONTR	Basic contributions for calculating the deficit tax rate	$= (.75*(TRBASIC_{-1} + TRREPLEN_{-1})*WSTX_{-1}) + (.25*(TRBASIC_{-2} + TRREPLEN_{-2})*WSTX_{-2}))$
DEFICIT	Deficit used in the numerator of the deficit tax rate calculation	$= FLOOR - RES930$
DEFRATIO	Deficit ratio	$= DEFICIT/BASCONTR$
TRDEFRAW	Deficit ratio tax rate, unconstrained	$= DEFRATIO*TRBASIC_{-1}$
TRDEFICT	Deficit ratio tax rate	$= Minimum(TRDEFRAW, 2.0)$, rounded to the nearest .01

CREDIT	Tax credit to employers when the fund balance exceeds 2 percent of taxable payroll	$= \text{RES930} - \text{CEILING}$
TRCREDIT	Credit tax rate subtracted from employer rate when reserves exceed the ceiling	$= 100*\text{CREDIT}/\text{WSTX}$
TRINTON	Interest tax in effect	$= 0$ (off) if RES930 >=0, otherwise $= 1$
TRINT	Tax rate for the interest tax	$= .2$ if TRINTON $= 1$, otherwise $= 0$
TRSMAX	Maximum statutory tax rate	$= 6.0 + (2.0*\text{DEFTAXON}) + \text{TRREPLN} + \text{TRINT} - \text{TRCREDIT}$
TRSMIN	Minimum statutory tax rate	$= \text{TRREPLN} + \text{TRINT}$
TREFF	Effective tax rate on taxable wages, percent	$= -.916 + 1.473*\text{BENRATIO} + .365*\text{RPLNRATO}$

$$-.916 + 1.473*\text{BENRATIO} + .365*\text{RPLNRATO}$$
$$(4.5) \quad (16.5) \quad\quad (3.0)$$
$$+.931*\text{TRSMIN} + .043*\text{TRSMAX}$$
$$(3.5) \quad\quad (2.2)$$
$$\bar{R}^2 = .982 \quad \text{S.E.} = .081 \quad \text{D.W.} = 1.92$$
Sample period $=$ 1963 to 1987

TAX	Total tax receipts	$= (\text{TREFF}/100)*\text{WSTX}$

BLOCK 4
INTEREST

INTRT	Interest rate on trust fund balances	Exogenous variable
RESNL	Net trust fund reserves at the end of last year	Predetermined variable
RESNHT	Initial estimate of trust fund balance, end of current year	$= \text{RESNL} + \text{TAX} - \text{BEN}$
RESNAV	Average trust fund balance for the year	$= (\text{RESNL} + \text{RESNHT})/2$
RESNPB	Average positive fund balance for the year	$= \text{RESNAV}$ if RESNAV > 0, otherwise $= 0$
INT	Interest income for the year	$= \text{INTRAT}*\text{RESNPB}$

BLOCK 5
FUND BALANCE

RESNL	Net trust fund reserves at the end of last year	Predetermined variable
TAX	Total tax payments	Endogenous variable, determined in Block 3
INT	Interest income for the year	Endogenous variable, determined in Block 4
BEN	Total benefit payments from the trust fund	Endogenous variable, determined in Block 2
RESNET	Net trust fund reserves at the end of the current year	$= \text{RESNL} + \text{TAX} + \text{INT} - \text{BEN}$

Appendix C
The Michigan Model

All variables used in the model of Michigan are defined in this appendix. Also shown are the behavioral equations and definitional relations that link the model's variables.

BLOCK 1
LABOR MARKET

GRCLF   Growth rate in the   Exogenous variable
         labor force, percent

GRAWW   Growth rate in average   Exogenous variable
         weekly wages, percent

INTRAT   Interest rate on trust   Exogenous variable
         fund balances, percent

TUR   Total unemployment rate,   Exogenous variable
         percent of labor force

CLF   Labor force $=(1+GRCLF/100)*CLF_{-1}$

TU   Total unemployment $= CLF*TUR/100$

ECPS   Total employment $= CLF - TU$

T67   Time trend starting   1967 = 1, 1968 =2, etc.
         in 1967

T79   Time trend starting   1979 = 1, 1980 = 2, etc.,
         in 1979   = 0 before 1979

RNXS   Real net exports as a   Exogenous variable
         percent of GNP

EMMT   Employment in mining, $= 1439.600\ -34.464*TUR\ +9.018*RNXS$
         manufacturing, and $(73.4)\quad (14.1)\quad\quad (1.9)$
         transportation $+13.380*T67\ -27.481*T79$
                $(1.7)\qquad (3.5)$

                         $\bar{R}^2 = .970$ S.E. = 17.547 D.W. = 2.07
                         Sample period 1967 to 1987

ETAX   Employment of taxable $= -718.962\ +.687*ECPS\ +.599*EMMT$
         covered employers $(8.6)\quad (39.2)\quad\quad (15.8)$
                $+ 87.946*D85$
                (6.9)

                         $\bar{R}^2 = .993$ S.E. = 16.288   D.W. = 2.39
                         Sample period 1967 to 1987
                         D85 = 1 from 1985 to 1987, = 0 otherwise

EREI   Employment of reimburs- $= 131.234\ +\ .040*ETAX\ +290.104*D75$
         able covered employers $(2.3)\quad (1.8)\quad\quad (27.3)$
                $+ 110.231*D78$
                (11.7)

                         $\bar{R}^2 = .993$ S.E. = 13.003 D.W. = 1.68
                         Sample period 1972 to 1987
                         D75 = 1 from 1975 to 1987, = 0 otherwise
                         D78 = 1 from 1978 to 1987, = 0 otherwise

ECOV	Employment covered by the UI program	$= ETAX + EREI$
AWW	Average weekly wages of taxable employers	$= (1 + GRAWW/100)*AWW_{-1}$

BLOCK 2
BENEFITS

IUTU	Ratio of insured to total unemployment	$= .4203 + .0207*TUR - .0182*TUR_{-1}$

$$\quad (12.8) \quad (4.2) \quad\quad (3.4)$$
$$- .1508*D81$$
$$\quad (5.0)$$

$\bar{R}^2 = .797 \quad S.E. = .0446 \quad D.W. = 2.24$
Sample period 1967 to 1987
D81 = 1 from 1981 to 1987, = 0 otherwise
Intercept adjustment = +.0502 from 1987

IU	Insured unemployment	$= IUTU*TU$
IUR	Ins unemployment rate	$= 100*IU/ECOV$
IUTXIU	Ratio of IU of taxable employers to total IU	Exogenous variable, $= .955$, average for 1983-1987
WBWCL	Ratio of weeks paid to weeks claimed	Exogenous variable, $= .879$, average for 1983-1987
MAXWBAC	Maximum weekly benefit, raw calculation	$= (.980*.580*(AWW_{-1} + AWW_{-2})/2) - .5$

.980 adjusts AWW to private AWW
.580 is the MAXWBA percentage

MAXWBA	Maximum weekly benefit	$= Round(MAXWBAC)$, to nearest dollar
MBAWW	Maximum weekly benefit as a proportion of average weekly wages	$= MAXWBA/AWW$
REPRATE	Replacement rate, ratio of weekly benefits to average weekly wages	$= .1701 + .4157*MBAWW + .00344*TUR$

$$\quad (8.2) \quad (6.2) \quad\quad\quad (2.5)$$
$$- .00370*TUR_{-1}$$
$$\quad (2.6)$$

$\bar{R}^2 = .804 \quad S.E. = .0120 \quad D.W. = 1.33$
Sample period 1967 to 1987
Intercept adjustment = -.02618 after 1986

WBA	Weekly benefit amount	$= REPRATE*AWW$
BENADJ	Benefit adjustment, adjusts product of benefit variables to agree with aggregate benefit payments in regular UI	Exogenous variable, $= .978$, average for 1983-1986
BENREG	Aggregate benefit payments for regular UI	$= IU*IUTXIU*WBWCL*WBA*BENADJ*(.052)$
EBON	Trigger to turn on the EB program	$= 1$ if IUR $\geq 4.0\%$, otherwise $= 0$
MOEBO3	EB program triggered on for 3 months	$= 3$ if $5.1\% >$ IUR $\geq 4.0\%$, otherwise $= 0$
MOEBO5	EB program triggered on for 5 months	$= 5$ if $5.3\% >$ IUR $\geq 5.1\%$, otherwise $= 0$

MOEB08	EB program triggered on for 8 months	= 8 if 5.4% > IUR ≥ 5.3%, otherwise = 0
MOEB10	EB program triggered on for 10 months	= 10 if 5.55% > IUR ≥ 5.4%, otherwise = 0
MOEB12	EB program triggered on for 12 months	= 12 if IUR ≥ 5.55%, otherwise = 0
MOEB	Months EB program is triggered on for the year	= MOEB03 + MOEB05 + MOEB08 + MOEB10 + MOEB12
APWKEB	Ratio of annualized weeks compensated in EB to weeks compensated in the regular UI program	= .311*EBON .311 = average proportion for the 1975-77 and 1980-82 periods
WBAEB	Weekly benefit amount for EB beneficiaries	= WBA
EBADJ	EB benefit adjustment, adjusts product of EB variables to agree with total EB payments	Exogenous variable, =.961, average for 1980-1982
EBTOT	Total EB payments	= (EBON − 1)*IU*IUTXIU*WBWCL*(MOEB/12)* APWKEB*WBAEB*EBADJ*(.052)
EBS	State share of EB costs	= EBTOT/2
BEN	Total benefit payments from the trust fund	= BENREG + EBS

BLOCK 3
TAXES

| TXBASE | Taxable wage base | Exogenous variable |
| TBAW | Ratio of the taxable wage base to average weekly wages | = TXBASE/(52*AWW) |

TWP   Taxable wage proportion

$$= -.0657 +.8158*TBAW +.4224*(EMMT/ECPS)$$
$$\quad (2.8) \quad (24.1) \quad\quad\quad (10.2)$$
$$+.00249*TUR -.00138*TUR_{-1}$$
$$\quad (3.8) \quad\quad (2.8)$$

$\overline{R}^2 = .992$ S.E. = .00390   D.W. = 1.71
Sample period 1967 to 1987

WSTAX	Taxable wages and salaries of taxable covered employers	= ETAX*AWW*TWP*(.052)/1000 (in $ billions)
WSTX331L	Taxable wages and salaries for year ending March 31 of last year	= (.25*WSTX_{-1}) + (.75*WSTX_{-2})
WSTO	Total wages and salaries of taxable covered employers	= ETAX*AWW*(.052)/1000 (in $ billions)

WSTO331L	Total wages and salaries of taxable employers for the year ending March 31 of last year	$= (.25*WSTO_{-1}) + (.75*WSTO_{-2})$
WSTO630L	Total wages and salaries of taxable employers for the year ending June 30 of last year	$= (WSTO_{-1} + WSTO_{-2})/2$
RESN630L	Net trust fund reserves on June 30 of last year	$= (RESNET_{-1} + RESNET_{-2})/2$ RESNET defined below
RR630L	Reserve ratio on June 30 of last year	$= 100*RESN630L/(WSTO630L*1000)$
WSTXCBC	Taxable wages and salaries for the chargable benefits component (CBC) of employer taxes	$= (.5*WSTX_{-1}) + WSTX_{-2} + WSTX_{-3} + WSTX_{-4} + WSTX_{-5} + (.5*WSTX_{-6})$
BENCBC	Benefits for the chargeable benefits component (CBC) of employer taxes	$= (.5*BEN_{-1}) + BEN_{-2} + BEN_{-3} + BEN_{-4} + BEN_{-5} + (.5*BEN_{-6})$
BRCBC	Benefit ratio for the chargeable benefits tax	$= 100*BENCBC/(WSTXCBC*1000)$, rounded to the next highest .1%
TRABC	Account building tax rate, maximum	$= 3\%$
TRNBCRAW	Noncharged benefits tax rate, raw calculation	$= 100*((.0375*WSTO331L*1000) - RESN630L)/(WSTX331L*1000)$
TRNBCC	Constrained NBC tax rate	$= Min(TRNBCRAW,1\%)$ if $TRNBCRAW >= 0$, otherwise $= 0$
TRNBC	Noncharged benefits tax rate	$=$ TRNBCC, rounded to the next highest .1%
TRSOLV	Solvency tax rate	$= 2\%$ if $RESN630L < 0$, otherwise $= 0$
TRSMIN	Minimum statutory tax rate	$=$ TRNBC
TRSMAX	Maximum statutory tax rate	$= 6\% + TRABC + TRNBC$
TREFF	Effective tax rate on taxable wages, percent	$= .6845 + .8336*TRSMIN +.6415*BRCBC$ (6.3) (5.0) (12.8)
		$\bar{R}^2 = .970$ S.E. $= .217$ D.W. $= 1.45$ Sample period 1963 to 1987
TAX	Total tax payments	$= WSTO*TWP*(TREFF/100)$

BLOCK 4
INTEREST

INTRT	Interest rate on trust fund balances	Exogenous variable
RESNL	Net trust fund reserves at the end of last year	Predetermined variable

RESNHT	Initial estimate of trust fund balance, end of current year	= RESNL + TAX - BEN
RESNAV	Average trust fund balance for the year	= (RESNL + RESNHT)/2
RESNPB	Average positive fund balance for the year	= RESNAV if RESNAV > 0, otherwise = 0
INT	Interest income for the year	= INTRT*RESNPB

BLOCK 5
FUND BALANCE

RESNL	Net trust fund reserves at the end of last year	Predetermined variable
TAX	Total tax payments	Endogenous variable, determined in Block 3
INT	Interest income for the year	Endogenous variable, determined in Block 4
BEN	Total benefit payments from the trust fund	Endogenous variable, determined in Block 2
RESNET	Net trust fund reserves at the end of the current year	= RESNL + TAX + INT - BEN

References

Barnow, Burt and Wayne Vroman, *An Analysis of UI Trust Fund Adequacy*. Unemployment Insurance Occasional Paper 87-1. Washington, D.C.: U.S. Department of Labor, 1987.

Baskin, Elba and Galen Hite, "Development of Theoretical and Empirical Measures of Unemployment Insurance Reserve Fund Adequacy." Report to the U.S. Department of Labor under contract No. 99-6-788-04-24, Oklahoma State University, College of Business Administration (September 1977).

Becker, Joseph, "Reinsurance and Cost Equalization," in *Unemployment Compensation: Studies and Research, Volume 2*. Washington, D.C.: GPO, 1980, pp. 349-354.

Bowes, Marianne, Frank Brechling and Kathleen Utgoff, "An Evaluation of UI Funds," in *Unemployment Compensation: Studies and Research, Volume 2*. Washington, D.C.: GPO, 1980, pp. 315-328.

Burtless, Gary, "Why is Insured Unemployment So Low? " *Brookings Papers on Economic Activity* 1 (1983), pp. 225-254.

Burtless, Gary and Daniel Saks, "The Decline in Insured Unemployment During the 1980s." Washington, D.C.: The Brookings Institution, March 1984.

Burtless, Gary and Wayne Vroman, "The Performance of Unemployment Insurance Since 1979," *Proceedings of the Industrial Relations Research Association*, Dallas, TX, December 28-30, 1984, pp. 138-146.

Corson, Walter et al., *The New Jersey Unemployment Insurance Reemployment Demonstration Project Final Evaluation Report*. Unemployment Insurance Occasional Paper 89-3. Washington, D.C.: U.S. Department of Labor, April 1989.

Corson, Walter and Walter Nicholson, *An Examination of Declining UI Claims During the 1980s*. Unemployment Insurance Occasional Paper 88-3. Washington, D.C.: U.S. Department of Labor, 1988.

Crosslin, Robert, "Cost Reinsurance," in *Unemployment Compensation: Studies and Research, Volume 2*. Washington, D.C.: GPO, 1980, pp. 355-367.

Freiman, Marc, "State Trust Fund Behavior," in *Unemployment Compensation: Studies and Research, Volume 2*. Washington, D.C.: GPO, 1980, pp. 299-313.

Fullerton, Howard, "The 1995 Labor Force: BLS' Latest Projections," *Monthly Labor Review* (November 1985), pp. 17-22.

Haber, William and Merrill Murray, *Unemployment Insurance in the American Economy*. Homewood, IL: Richard D. Irwin, 1966.

Interstate Conference of Emplyment Security Agencies, "Report of Committee on Benefit Financing." Washington, D.C.: Interstate Conference of Employment Security Agencies, August 1959.

LeBlond, Geoffrey and Douglass Cobb, *Using 123*, Second Edition. Indianapolis, IN: Que Corporation, 1985.

Mercer Associates, "State Unemployment Insurance User's Manual for Projection Program and Financial Forecast Program," Two Volumes. Prepared for Division of Actuarial Services, UI Service, U.S. Department of Labor (July 1977).

National Foundation for Unemployment Compensation and Workers' Compensation, "Highlights of State Unemployment Compensation Laws, January 1988." Washington, D.C., 1988.

South Carolina Employment Security Commission, "The Development of an Adequate Taxing System for Financing Unemployment Insurance." Columbia, SC: South Carolina Employment Security Commission, August 1976.

U.S. Department of Labor, Bureau of Labor Statistics, "Geographic Profile of Employment and Unemployment, 1987." Bulletin 2305. Washington, D.C.: GPO, April 1988a.

U.S. Department of Labor, Employment and Training Administration, *Unemployment Insurance Financial Data,* ET Handbook 394. Washington, D.C.: U.S. Department of Labor, 1983

U.S. Department of Labor, UI Service, "Reserve Adequacy." Unemployment Insurance Program Letter No. 44–81. Washington, D.C.: U.S. Department of Labor, October 13, 1981.

U.S. Department of Labor, UI Service, " Title XII Advances and Repayments as of December 31, 1987." Washington, D.C.: U.S. Department of Labor, February 11, 1988b.

U.S. Executive Office of the President, *Economic Report of the President, 1988.* Washington, D.C.: GPO, February 1988.

U.S. General Accounting Office, "Unemployment Insurance Trust Fund Reserves Inadequate," Report HRD–88–55. Washington, D.C.: U.S. General Accounting Office, September 26, 1988.

U.S. House of Representatives, "Reform of the Unemployment Compensation Program." Hearings before the Subcommittee on Public Assistance and Unemployment Compensation, Committee on Ways and Means, Series 100–46. Washington, D.C.: GPO, December 14, 1987.

Vroman, Wayne, "The Aggregate Performance of Unemployment Insurance, 1980 to 1985," in W. Lee Hansen and James Byers, eds., *The Second Half Century of Unemployment Insurance: Lessons from the Past.* Madison, WI: University of Wisconsin Press, 1990, pp. 19–46.

Vroman, Wayne, *The Funding Crisis in State Unemployment Insurance.* Kalamazoo, MI: W.E. Upjohn Institute, 1986.

Vroman, Wayne, *UISIM: A Simulation Model of Unemployment Insurance.* Washington, D.C.: The Urban Institute, April 1987.

INDEX

174

Florida: debt-free status of, 15, 16; fund adequacy simulation analysis, 81-115; size of trust fund, 37; UISIM simulation model, 79-80
Flow-based systems. *See* Experience rating systems
Freiman, Marc, 53-54, 59
Fullerton, Howard, 74
FUT. *See* Federal Unemployment Tax (FUT)
FUTA. *See* Federal Unemployment Tax Act (FUTA)

Haber, William, 1, 61nn4, 13
Hawaii, 37
Hite, Galen, 57-58, 59

ICESA. *See* Interstate Conference of Employment Security Agencies (ICESA)
Illinois: debt of, 15; unemployment insurance statute of, 38
Indexation, state, 84, 88
Inflation: effect of high, 4; simulation analysis with, 95-98
Insolvency: risk of, 36, 38, 42-43, 51-59; *See also* Experience rating systems; Solvency tax
Insured unemployment rate (IUR), 66, 71, 122
Insured unemployment to total unemployment ratio (IU/TU), 11-17, 70; decline in, 11-17; in Massachusetts, 75
Interest income: effect in reserve ratio versus benefit ratio of, 101-2; in trust fund receipts, 37, 90; for UI trust fund, 33
Interstate Conference of Employment Security Agencies (ICESA), 44-45
IUR. *See* Insured unemployment rate (IUR)
IU/TU. *See* Insured unemployment to total unemployment ratio (IU/TU)

Kansas, 37

Labor market performance: effect on borrowing patterns: New Jersey, 136-38; effect on borrowing patterns of, 136-40; influences on, 133, 136; regional analysis of, 121-30; *See also* Employment share, regional; Unemployment
LeBlond, Geoffrey, 65
Loan repayment, 1-7, 17-19, 22-29; *See also* Loans; Penalty tax, federal
Loans: interest-bearing, 19, 22-29, 60; interest-free, 2, 4-7, 19, 22-24, 27-29; long-term, large-scale, 1-7, 43, 81; *See also* Borrowing patterns, regional; Borrowing patterns, state
LOTUS spreadsheets, 63-67
Louisiana, 39

Massachusetts: debt status of, 15, 16, 27, 139; specialized solvency tax of, 78-79, 106; UISIM simulation model in, 73-79, 153-58; UISIM solvency analysis for, 73-79
Mercer Associates, 63
Michigan: debt of, 6, 15, 27, 82, 139; fund adequacy simulation analysis, 81-115; loans to, 2; solvency tax in, 106-7; UISIM model for, 165-69; UISIM simulation model in, 79-80, 165-69
Minnesota, 27
Mississippi, 37
Modeling, simulation, 63
Montana, 27
Murray, Merrill, 1, 61nn4, 13